Reach the Highest Standard in Professional Learning: Implementation

Volumes in the Reach the Highest Standard in Professional Learning Series

Learning Communities

Leadership

Resources

Data

Learning Designs

Implementation

Outcomes

Reach the Highest Standard in Professional Learning: Implementation

Michael Fullan
Shirley M. Hord
Valerie von Frank

A Joint Publication

CORWIN
A SAGE Company

learningforward

CORWIN
A SAGE Company

FOR INFORMATION:

Corwin
A SAGE Company
2455 Teller Road
Thousand Oaks, California 91320
(800) 233-9936
www.corwin.com

SAGE Publications Ltd.
1 Oliver's Yard
55 City Road
London EC1Y 1SP
United Kingdom

SAGE Publications India Pvt. Ltd.
B 1/I 1 Mohan Cooperative Industrial Area
Mathura Road, New Delhi 110 044
India

SAGE Publications Asia-Pacific Pte. Ltd.
3 Church Street
#10-04 Samsung Hub
Singapore 049483

Acquisitions Editor: Dan Alpert
Associate Editor: Kimberly Greenberg
Editorial Assistant: Cesar Reyes
Production Editor: Cassandra Margaret Seibel
Copy Editor: Sarah J. Duffy
Typesetter: C&M Digitals (P) Ltd.
Proofreader: Caryne Brown
Indexer: Sheila Bodell
Cover Designer: Gail Buschman
Marketing Manager: Stephanie Trkay

Printed in the United States of America.

Library of Congress Cataloging-in-Publication Data

Fullan, Michael.
Reach the highest standard in professional learning: implementation/Michael Fullan, Shirley M. Hord, Valerie von Frank.

pages cm.
Includes bibliographical references and index.

ISBN 978-1-4522-9189-5 (pbk. : alk. paper)
1. Teachers—In-service training—Standards.
2. Professional learning communities.
I. Hord, Shirley M. II. Von Frank, Valerie. III. Title.

LB1731.F86 2015
370.71'1—dc23 2014022858

This book is printed on acid-free paper.

SFI Certified Sourcing
www.sfiprogram.org
SFI-00453
SFI label applies to text stock

14 15 16 17 18 10 9 8 7 6 5 4 3 2 1

Contents

Introduction to the Series

These are the demands on educators and school systems right now, among many others:

- They must fulfill the moral imperative of educating every child for tomorrow's world, regardless of background or status.
- They must be prepared to implement college- and career-ready standards and related assessments.
- They must implement educator evaluations tied to accountability systems.

A critical element in creating school systems that can meet these demands is building the capacity of the system's educators at all levels, from the classroom teacher to the instructional coach to the school principal to the central office administrator, and including those partners who work within and beyond districts. Building educator capacity in this context requires effective professional learning.

Learning Forward's Standards for Professional Learning define the essential elements of and conditions for professional learning that leads to changed educator practices and improved student results. They are grounded in the understanding that the ultimate purpose of professional learning is increasing student success. Educator effectiveness—and this includes all educators working in and with school systems, not just teachers—is linked closely to student learning. Therefore increasing the effectiveness of educators is a key lever to school improvement.

Effective professional learning happens in a culture of continuous improvement, informed by data about student and educator performance and supported by leadership and sufficient resources.

Educators learning daily have access to information about relevant instructional strategies and resources and, just as important, time for collaboration with colleagues, coaches, and school leaders. Education leaders and systems that value effective professional learning provide not only sufficient time and money but also create structures that reinforce monitoring and evaluation of that learning so they understand what is effective and have information to adjust and improve.

Why Standards?

Given that any system can—and must—develop expertise about professional learning, why are standards important? Among many reasons are these:

First, adherence to standards ensures equity. When learning leaders across schools and systems agree to follow a common set of guidelines, they are committing to equal opportunities for all the learners in those systems. If all learning is in alignment with the Standards for Professional Learning and tied to student and school improvement goals, then all educators have access to the best expertise available to improve their practice and monitor results.

Standards also provide a common language that allows for conversation, collaboration, and implementation planning that crosses state, regional, and national borders. This collaboration can leverage expertise from any corner of the world to change practice and results.

Finally, standards offer guidelines for accountability. While an endorsement of the standards doesn't in itself guarantee quality, they provide a framework within which systems can establish measures to monitor progress, alignment, and results.

From Standards to Transformation

So a commitment to standards is a first critical step. Moving into deep understanding and sustained implementation of standards is another matter. Transforming practices, and indeed, whole systems, will require long-term study, planning, and evaluation.

Reach the Highest Standard in Professional Learning is created to be an essential set of tools to help school and system leaders take those steps. As with the Standards for Professional Learning themselves, there will be seven volumes, one for each standard.

While the standards were created to work in synergy, we know that educators approach professional learning from a wide range of experiences, concerns, expertise, and passions. Perhaps a school leader may have started PLCs in his school to address a particular learning challenge, and thus has an abiding interest in how learning communities can foster teacher quality and better results. Maybe a central office administrator started her journey to standards-based professional learning through a study of how data informs changes, and she wants to learn more about the foundations of data use. This series was created to support such educators and to help them continue on their journey of understanding systemwide improvement and the pieces that make such transformation possible.

In developing this series of books on the Standards for Professional Learning, Corwin and Learning Forward envisioned that practitioners would enter this world of information through one particular book, and that their needs and interests would take them to all seven as the books are developed. The intention is to serve the range of needs practitioners bring and to support a full understanding of the elements critical to effective professional learning.

All seven volumes in Reach the Highest Standard in Professional Learning share a common structure, with components to support knowledge development, exploration of changes in practice, and a vision of each concept at work in real-world settings.

In each volume, readers will find

- A think piece developed by a leading voice in the professional learning field. These thought leaders represent both scholars and practitioners, and their work invites readers to consider the foundations of each standard and to push understanding of those seven standards.
- An implementation piece that helps readers put the think piece and related ideas into practice, with tools for both individuals and groups to use in reflection and discussion about the standards. Shirley M. Hord and Patricia Roy, longstanding Learning Forward standards leaders, created the implementation pieces across the entire series.
- A case study that illuminates what it looks like in schools and districts when education leaders prioritize the standards in

their improvement priorities. Valerie von Frank, with many years of writing about education in general and professional learning in particular, reported these pieces, highlighting insights specific to each standard.

Moving Toward Transformation

We know this about effective professional learning: Building awareness isn't enough to change practice. It's a critical first piece, and these volumes will help in knowledge development. But sustaining knowledge and implementing change require more.

Our intention is that the content and structure of the volumes move readers from awareness to changes in practice to transformation of systems. And of course transformation requires much more. Commitment to a vision for change is an exciting place to start. A long-term informed investment of time, energy, and resources is nonnegotiable, as is leadership that transcends one visionary leader who will inevitably move on.

Ultimately, it will be the development of a culture of collective responsibility for all students that sustains improvement. We invite you to begin your journey toward developing that culture through study of the Standards for Professional Learning and through Reach the Highest Standard in Professional Learning. Learning Forward will continue to support the development of knowledge, tools, and evidence that inform practitioners and the field. Next year's challenges may be new ones, and educators working at their full potential will always be at the core of reaching our goals for students.

Stephanie Hirsh
Executive Director, Learning Forward

The Learning Forward Standards for Professional Learning

Learning Communities: Professional learning that increases educator effectiveness and results for all students occurs within learning communities committed to continuous improvement, collective responsibility, and goal alignment.

Leadership: Professional learning that increases educator effectiveness and results for all students requires skillful leaders who develop capacity, advocate, and create support systems for professional learning.

Resources: Professional learning that increases educator effectiveness and results for all students requires prioritizing, monitoring, and coordinating resources for educator learning.

Data: Professional learning that increases educator effectiveness and results for all students uses a variety of sources and types of student, educator, and system data to plan, assess, and evaluate professional learning.

Learning Designs: Professional learning that increases educator effectiveness and results for all students integrates theories, research, and models of human learning to achieve its intended outcomes.

Implementation: Professional learning that increases educator effectiveness and results for all students applies research on change and sustains support for implementation of professional learning for long-term change.

Outcomes: Professional learning that increases educator effectiveness and results for all students aligns its outcomes with educator performance and student curriculum standards.

Source: Learning Forward. (2011). *Standards for Professional Learning.* Oxford, OH: Author.

The Implementation Standard

Professional learning that increases educator effectiveness and results for all students *applies research on change and sustains support for implementation of professional learning for long-term change.*

The primary goals for professional learning are changes in educator practice and increases in student learning. This is a process that occurs over time and requires support for implementation to embed the new learning into practices. Those responsible for professional learning apply findings from change process research to support long-term change in practice by extending learning over time. They integrate a variety of supports for individuals, teams, and schools. Finally, they integrate constructive feedback and reflection to support continuous improvement in practice that allows educators to move along a continuum from novice to expert through application of their professional learning.

Apply Change Research

Effective professional learning integrates research about individual, organization, technical, and adaptive change through supporting and sustaining implementation for long-term change. Those responsible for professional learning, whether leaders, facilitators, or participants, commit to long-term change by setting clear goals and maintaining high expectations for implementation with fidelity. Drawing from multiple bodies of research about change, leaders provide and align resources, including time, staff, materials, and technology, to initiate and sustain implementation. Individuals, peers, coaches, and leaders use tools and metrics to gather evidence to monitor and assess implementation. Leaders and coaches model salient practices and maintain a sustained focus on the goals and strategies for achieving them. Leaders create and maintain a culture of support by encouraging stakeholders to use data to identify implementation challenges and engage them in identifying and recommending ongoing refinements to increase results. They engender community support for implementation by communicating incremental successes, reiterating goals, and honestly discussing the complexities of deep change.

Understanding how individuals and organizations respond to change and how various personal, cognitive, and work environment factors affect those experiencing change gives those leading, facilitating, or participating in professional learning the ability to differentiate support, tap educators' strengths and talents, and increase educator effectiveness and student learning.

Sustain Implementation

Professional learning produces changes in educator practice and student learning when it sustains implementation support over time. Episodic, periodic, or occasional professional learning has little effect on educator practice or student learning because it rarely includes ongoing support or opportunities for extended learning to support implementation. Formal professional learning, such as online, on-site, or hybrid workshops, conferences, or courses, is useful to develop or expand knowledge and skills, share emerging ideas, and network learners with one another. To bridge the knowing-doing gap and integrate new ideas into practice, however, educators need three to five years of ongoing implementation support that includes opportunities to deepen their understanding and address problems associated with practice.

Ongoing support for implementation of professional learning takes many forms and occurs at the implementation site. It may be formalized through ongoing workshops designed to deepen understanding and refine educator practice. It occurs through coaching, reflection, or reviewing results. It may occur individually, in pairs, or in collaborative learning teams when educators plan, implement, analyze, reflect, and evaluate the integration of their professional learning into their practice. It occurs within learning communities that meet to learn or refine instructional strategies; plan lessons that integrate the new strategies; share experiences about implementing those lessons; analyze student work together to reflect on the results of use of the strategies; and assess their progress toward their defined goals. School- and system-based coaches provide extended learning opportunities, resources for implementation, demonstrations of the practices, and specific, personalized guidance. Peer support groups, study groups, peer observation, co-teaching, and co-planning are other examples of extended support. When educators work to resolve challenges related to integration of professional learning, they support and sustain implementation. Professional learning is a process of continuous improvement focused on achieving clearly defined student and educator learning goals rather than an event defined by a predetermined number of hours.

Provide Constructive Feedback

Constructive feedback accelerates implementation by providing formative assessment through the learning and implementation process. It provides specific information to assess practice in relationship to established expectations and to adjust practice so that it more closely aligns with those expectations. Feedback from peers, coaches, supervisors, external experts, students, self, and others offers information for educators to use as they refine practices. Reflection is another form of feedback in which a learner engages in providing constructive feedback on his or her own or others' practices.

Effective feedback is based on clearly defined expected behaviors, acknowledges progress toward expectations, and provides guidance for achieving full implementation. Giving and receiving feedback about successes and improvements require skillfulness in clear, nonjudgmental communication based on evidence, commitment to continuous improvement and shared goals, and trusting, respectful relationships between those giving and receiving feedback.

To add validity and reliability to the feedback process, educators develop and use common, clear expectations that define practice so that the feedback is focused, objective, relevant, valid, and purposeful.

Educators consider and decide what evidence best demonstrates the expected practices and their results. Frequent feedback supports continuous improvement, whereas occasional feedback is often considered evaluative. Feedback about progress toward expected practices provides encouragement to sustain the desired changes over time. Tools that define expected behaviors facilitate data collection and open, honest feedback.

Source: Learning Forward. (2011). *Standards for Professional Learning.* Oxford, OH: Author.

About the Authors

An innovative thinker who is sought after by institutions, publishers, and international think tanks, **Michael Fullan** is special advisor on education to the premier and the minister of education of Ontario. He formerly served as dean and professor emeritus at the Ontario Institute for Studies in Education at the University of Toronto. He holds honorary doctorates from the University of Edinburgh, in Scotland, and from Nipissing University, in Canada.

Fullan served as dean of the faculty of education at the University of Toronto from 1988 to 2003, leading two major organizational transformations, including a merger of two large schools of education. He is currently working as adviser and consultant on several major education reform initiatives around the world.

He bases his work on research and practice in both the public and private sectors, finding an increasing convergence in this literature. He has written several best sellers on leadership and change that have been translated into several languages. Four of his books have won book of the year awards, and his publications have been translated into several languages. Learn more about his work at www.michaelfullan.ca.

Now Michael Fullan is offering his experience to you in an eStudy opportunity! Visit www.corwin.com/learning/estudy/fullan.html for more information.

Dr. Shirley M. Hord, PhD, is the scholar laureate of Learning Forward (previously National Staff Development Council), following her retirement as Scholar Emerita at the Southwest Educational Development Laboratory in Austin, Texas. There she directed the Strategies for Increasing Student Success Program. She continues to design and coordinate professional development activities related to educational change and improvement, school leadership, and the creation of professional learning communities.

Her early roles as elementary school classroom teacher and as a member of the university science education faculty at The University of Texas at Austin were followed by her appointment as co-director of Research on the Improvement Process at the Research and Development Center for Teacher Education at The University of Texas at Austin. There she administered and conducted research on school improvement and the role of school leaders in school change.

She served as a fellow of the National Center for Effective Schools Research and Development and was U.S. representative to the Foundation for the International School Improvement Project, an international effort that develops research, training, and policy initiatives to support local school improvement practices.

In addition to working with educators at all levels across the U.S. and Canada, Hord makes presentations and consults in Asia, Europe, Australia, Africa, and Mexico.

Her current interests focus on the creation and functioning of educational organizations as learning communities and the role of leaders who serve such organizations. Dr. Hord is the author of numerous articles and books, of which a selection of the most recent are *Implementing Change: Patterns, Principles, and Potholes*, 4th ed. (with Gene E. Hall, 2015); *Reclaiming Our Teaching Profession: The Power of Educators Learning in Community* (with Edward F. Tobia, 2012); and *A Playbook for Professional Learning: Putting the Standards Into Action* (with Stephanie Hirsh, 2012).

Valerie von Frank is an author, editor, and communications consultant. A former newspaper editor and education reporter, she has focused much of her writing on education issues, including professional learning. She served as communications director in an urban school district and a nonprofit school reform organization and was the editor of *JSD,* the flagship magazine for the National Staff Development Council, now Learning Forward, for 7 years. She has written extensively for education publications, including *JSD, Tools for Schools, The Learning System, The Learning Principal,* and *T3.* She is coauthor with Ann Delehant of *Making Meetings Work: How to Get Started, Get Going, and Get It Done* (Corwin, 2007), with Linda Munger of *Change, Lead, Succeed* (National Staff Development Council, 2010), with Robert Garmston of *Unlocking Group Potential to Improve Schools* (Corwin, 2012), and with Jennifer Abrams of *The Multigenerational Workplace: Communicate, Collaborate, and Create Community* (Corwin, 2014).

CHAPTER ONE

Implementing the Implementation Standard

Michael Fullan

In this chapter we will examine what happens, or might happen, to a standard—in this case a standard for professional learning. We first examine the standard, then consider the failure of professional development, move to analyzing some promising examples of success, and conclude by recommending what would have to be done to implement the implementation standard. Essentially, the solution involves realizing that professional learning requires changes in the nature of professional learning *and* changes in the culture and context within which learning occurs.

LEARNING FORWARD'S IMPLEMENTATION STANDARD

The sixth of seven Professional Learning Standards focuses on implementation:

> Implementation: Professional learning that increases educator effectiveness and results for all students applies research on change and sustains support for implementation of professional learning for long-term change.

I grew up professionally with the concept of implementation. When I was completing my dissertation in the late 1960s, the term *implementation* was not yet used. In the 1960s the key ideas revolved around innovation. New math, team teaching, new science and social studies curriculum, open plan schools, and so on were expected to sweep the schools in the United States, all for the betterment of learning for all students. All went well until someone asked, "What is actually happening in classrooms?" One of the first books on the topic was John Goodlad and colleagues' (1970) *Behind the Classroom Door.* These researchers investigated eight trends (innovations) of the day by going into classrooms to observe the reality of practice. Not only did they find that teachers who claimed that they were using a given innovation actually were not doing so (it was not deception; they thought they were using it), but they also discovered teachers who had no idea they were employing a practice on the list, but were in fact implementing it! Welcome to the world of implementation.

There followed several studies, such as Neal Gross, Joseph Giacquinta, and Marilyn Bernstein's (1971) *Implementing Organizational Innovations,* Seymour Sarason's (1971) classic *The Culture of the School and the Problem of Change,* and our own "Research on Curriculum and Instruction Implementation" (Fullan & Pomfret, 1977). The emperor simply had no clothes—whatever was supposed to be happening was not evident. This has turned out to be a persistent problem (for which the standard is presumably a partial solution). We can skip a few decades—getting on to be half a century later and we find that in some respects the more things change, the more they remain the same. Stanford's Larry Cuban (2013) has been tracking implementation for the past 45 years and recently published the culmination of his research under the revealing title of *Inside the Black Box of Classroom Practice: Change Without Reform in American Education.* Cuban describes waves of structural reform—new curriculum, massive infusion of funds, strengthening accountability, standards, assessment, technology—you name it. And yet day-to-day classroom practice and corresponding student learning have barely budged.

In my own work on implementation, summarized in the 4th (on the way to the 5th) edition of *The New Meaning of Educational Change* (Fullan, 2007), I began to get at part of the problem by defining implementation as "putting into practice a new idea" (wherever the source of the idea). And implementation itself I said was a function of using "new materials, changing beliefs, developing new knowledge and skills, and changing behaviors." It was easy to engage in surface change without knowing it—changes in curriculum materials without changes in practice, or changes in practice without grasping the underlying beliefs. In addition, it is necessary to take into account all those factors that would affect the likelihood of implementation, such as leadership, culture, and indeed professional learning.

But for the purposes of the rest of this chapter, I think we can open the black box by simply stating that *implementation is professional learning.* Yes, professional learning that increases teacher effectiveness in terms of reaching all students. The standard itself is quite powerful. It calls for professional learning of best ideas that increases teacher effectiveness as a continuous learning proposition that keeps on giving. In short, it calls for a process of sustained development that pays off for teachers and students.

I am going to focus on effective practices, which when identified and leveraged, draw on the best of research. I will not directly examine how professional learning can learn more systematically from research. Implicit in what I am saying is that professional learning is best served by learning from other professionals and their practice, with *all parties* plugged into the evolving research base that stimulates effective practice.

A good place to start, then, one would think, is to invest in the professional learning of teachers so that they can learn and improve. It turns out that implementing the implementation plan is a lot more complex than we thought.

The Failure of Professional Development

This is not the place to do a review of research on professional development (PD) but I will state the conclusion at the outset and use three major studies a confirmation. I should say that many of the examples in the literature look like they have the bases covered—well funded, plenty of PD, lofty inspiring goals, committed leadership, and so on—and they still fail. First the conclusion: *Most PD fails to impact classroom practice and student learning.* In this statement I exclude the obvious problems of one-shot workshops, lack of follow-through, externally mandated training, and the like.

The three good examples are Cohen and Hill's (2001) math reform in California; Borman and associates' (2005) investigation of math and science reform in Chicago, El Paso, Memphis, and Miami; and the Cross City Campaign for Urban School Reform's (2005) evaluation of reforms in Chicago, Milwaukee, and Seattle (these examples are adapted from Fullan, Hill, & Crevola, 2006).

Cohen and Hill (2001) argue correctly that ongoing teacher learning is the key to linking new conceptions of instructional practice with assessment and improvement of student learning. They note that the policy—math reform—was intended to create coherence among elements of curriculum, assessment, and learning opportunities for teachers, but in reality,

> such coherence is rare in the blizzard of often divergent professional development that typically blows over U.S. public schools. Only a modest fraction of California elementary teachers—roughly 10 percent—has these experiences. Standards, assessments and accountability are more likely to succeed if they are accompanied by extended opportunities that are grounded in practice. (pp. 9–10)

So, problem one: Extended learning opportunities in relation to given practices exist for only a small minority of teachers—and even for this 10% there is no guarantee that learning would be continuous.

Confirmation of limited impact despite major focus and resources comes from Borman and associates' (2005) research. Each of the three cities received $15 million from the National Science Foundation's Urban Systemic Initiative. The strategy seemed to have all the right elements: a curriculum focus, a systemic orientation, plenty of investment in professional development, and an advanced conception of math and science learning. The policy documents state: "Instruction should emphasize active learning and higher-order thinking skills while providing investigative and problem-solving opportunities for all students" (p. 4). In addition, "both district and school administrators viewed the provision of professional development opportunities as a primary focus for reform implementation" (p. 216).

Borman et al. (2005) found that despite these favorable conditions, including basing professional development sessions on extensive modeling of the new pedagogy, little change in classrooms ensued: "only tenuous links [were identified] between professional development and classroom instruction" (p. 70). In their overall sample, they found through classroom observation that 78% of teaching remained teacher centered, with less than 6% student centered (p. 98). They conclude: "We are left with the unhappy reality that current professional development activities are not translating into the classroom with effective instructional strategies and content" (p. 153).

Finally, let's consider the Cross City Campaign (2005) initiative that consists of extensive case studies of Chicago, Milwaukee, and Seattle. All three systems have the support of political leaders and administrators, focused on many of the "right things," such as literacy and math, and used choice change strategies such as assessment for learning, professional development sessions, and new leadership and a systemwide commitment. Here is the conclusion of the case study evaluators: Despite the availability of huge major resources, the authority to carry out implementation, and the organizational changes designed to support instruction, "districts were unable to improve practice on any scale" (p. 4). Another conclusion, ominous for Common Core State Standards, I would say: "The recent effort to become a standards-based district was one of the first sustained instructional efforts with direct attention to teaching and learning. However, the conversations that district leaders had about standards *were rarely connected to changes in instruction*" (p. 69, italics added).

In all these examples we are talking about good ideas, well resourced with curriculum materials, and professional development funds in which PD is a central tenet of the reform strategy. As the Cross City Campaign (2005) researchers conclude, the strength of individual professional development offerings was quite high, but there was no overarching umbrella to integrate them (p. 80). My conclusion, which will become clearer in the rest of this chapter, is that *professional development is not necessarily professional learning.* For the latter to occur, the work of teachers must be embedded in a culture of learning.

Promising Examples

We can now turn the corner and start building the case for meaningful implementation of LF's Standard on Professional Learning. The key to understanding this standard is that, to be effective, professional learning must be embedded in *the day-to-day cultures of schools, districts, and the larger system.* We can lay the ground for this work by being clear about what research has been telling us for some time now in relation to this phenomenon. We need to address both the school level and the system level. Figure 1.1 portrays the full model. For professional learning to be most productive, it must be embedded in a culture of learning that has three levels: collaborative schools, collaborative district cultures, and system policies and strategies that expect, push for, and support learning as an ongoing feature of improving instructional practice linked to student learning and achievement.

School Level

I start by examining the relationship between the role of the principal and the condition for teacher learning because the latter is maximized when the principal focuses directly on how to enable

Figure 1.1 Embedded Professional Learning (PL)

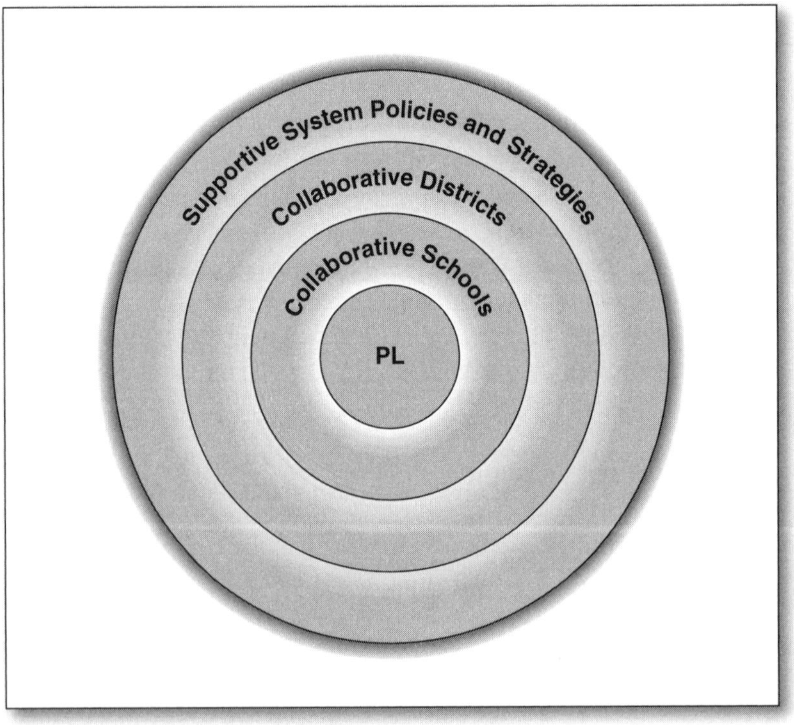

teachers to learn from each other in order to improve instructional effectiveness. Viviane Robinson and her colleagues conducted a large-scale Best Evidence Synthesis (BES) of research on the impact of school principals on student achievement. Robinson (2011) summarizes their conclusions in a book titled *Student-Centered Leadership.* They found five leadership domains that had significant effect sizes (in parentheses) on student achievement:

1. Establishing goals and expectations (0.42)
2. Resourcing strategically (0.31)
3. Ensuring quality teaching (0.42)
4. Leading teacher learning and development (0.84)
5. Ensuring an orderly and safe environment (0.27)

We get our first clue about professional learning in situ when we see that the one factor that stands out (twice as powerful as any other) is *leading teacher learning and development.* Thus what is needed is a culture that creates and fosters the conditions for purposeful ongoing learning on the part of teachers.

Helen Timperley (2011), Robinson's colleague at the University of Auckland and a longtime researcher on professional learning, conducted a parallel BES study on teacher learning, examining research on the relationship between teacher learning and student achievement. She drew similar conclusions: "Coherence across professional learning environments was not achieved through the completion of checklists and scripted lessons but rather through creating learning situations" where teachers and leaders learned together (p. 104).

Ken Leithwood (2012) at the University of Toronto, Karen Seashore Louis at the University of Minnesota, and others form another group who studied the conditions for teacher learning over the last four decades. They conclude that principals who develop collective leadership in the school focused on instruction, including teacher knowledge/skills and motivation, as well as on working conditions (such as time for collaboration) have the greatest impact on student achievement. In a nutshell, " leadership affects student learning when it is targeted at working relationships, improving instruction and indirectly student achievement" (p. 234).

Bryk, Bender-Sebring, Allensworth, Luppescu, and Easton's (2010) longitudinal research on over 200 elementary schools in Chicago is especially informative for our purposes. In a microcosm comparison of two schools that started out at similar levels of low performance, one school (Hancock) improved significantly over a 6-year period compared to the other school (Alexander). The difference:

> Strong principal leadership at Hancock School fostered the development of a vigorous professional community that was both actively reaching out to parents and sustaining a focus on improving instruction. In contrast, reform efforts at Alexander remained fragmented, suffering from both poor coordination and a lack of follow through. (p. 40)

There were major reform activities at both schools, but Alexander actually lost ground in reading by 9% and made no improvement in math over the years, while Hancock gained 10% in reading and 19% in math. We are talking about just two schools, but fortunately Bryk et al. (2010) have data on nearly all of the 477 elementary schools in Chicago.

When we consider the comprehensive picture, comparing the 100 or so schools that made significant progress compared to their peer schools that did not progress, we see a familiar (to this chapter) picture. The key explanation was school leadership as the driver for change, which in turn focused on the development of four interrelated forces: the professional capacity of teachers (individually and collectively), school climate (safe and orderly in the aid of learning), parent and community ties, and what they call the "instructional guidance system" (instructional practices that engage students in relation to key learning goals) as these affected each and every classroom (p. 62). Once again we see the development of the ongoing professional capacity of teachers—their continuous professional learning as a group is central to success.

In our recent work on professional capital, Andy Hargreaves and I have been even more explicit about the conditions at the school level that are essential for continuous professional learning. We see professional capital as the key to scaling up change efforts from individuals to groups to schools and districts. Professional capital is a function of the interaction of three components: human capital, social capital, and decisional capital. In the principal's case, *human capital* refers to the human resource or personnel dimension of the quality of teachers in the school—their basic teaching talents. Recruiting and cultivating the skills of individual teachers are one dimension of the principal's role. *Social capital* concerns the level of quality and quantity of interactions and relationships among people. Social capital in a school affects teachers' access to knowledge and information; their senses of expectation, obligation, and trust; and their commitment to work together for a common cause. *Decisional (or decision-making) capital* refers to the sum of practice and expertise in making decisions that may be spread across many individuals or groups in a school and its community. Decisional capital is that which is required for making good decisions—in our case, especially decisions about how to put human and social capital to work for achieving the goals of the school.

This three-part conception of professional capital can be used as a way of organizing one's roles in leading learning. In effect, the role of school leaders is to build professional capital across and beyond the school. All three must be addressed explicitly and in combination.

More confirmation of the more powerful alternative of combining human and social capital comes from studies by professor Carrie Leana (2011), a management professor at University of Pittsburgh with strong credentials in learning research. She claims, as I do here, that commonly touted change strategies typically err in trusting too much in the power of individuals to solve educational problems, while failing to enlist and capitalize on the power of the group. Just hire great teachers, great principals, and the problem will be solved.

In a straightforward study of elementary schools in New York City, Leana measured only three main variables:

- Human capital—by gathering information on the classroom experience and qualifications of individual teachers
- Social capital—by asking questions such as "To what extent do you work with other teachers in the school in a focused collaborative way to improve learning for students?"
- Math achievement over a 1-year period

While Leana found that teachers with greater human capital did get better math results, the teachers who got the greatest gains for their students were good at math teaching *and* worked with peers regularly to improve what they were doing and what they could learn from each other. She also found that teachers with lower skills who happened to be working in a school with high social capital got better results. The worst scenario was when both human and social capital were low.

Human capital should not be thought of as the main driver for developing the school. While it's true that, in situations where teacher quality is extremely low, bringing in great leaders (high individual human capital) is essential for beginning a turnaround process, little meaningful change results unless and until social capital enables the group to get its act together. Once you get started, social capital (the group) improves individuals more readily than individuals improve the group. For example, it is very hard for a weak teacher who enters a highly collaborative school to remain there without improving. Conversely, a highly talented individual will not remain in a noncollaborative school for very long. To paraphrase the post–Great War hit about Paris, "How you gonna keep 'em down on the farm, after they seen *the farm?!*" Good people will not stay at places that are unproductive.

Ultimately, we need both human and social capital, and we need the group to change the group for the better. The principal who spends a lot of time at the individual level, as current strategies demand, has less time to spend fostering group work and thereby building social capital with and among teachers and with the community and other sources of external support. How's the following for a finding?

> When principals spent more time building external social capital [with the community, and seeking other sources of ideas], the quality of instruction in the school was higher and students' scores on standardized tests in both reading and math were higher. Conversely, principals spending more time on mentoring and monitoring teachers had no effect on teacher social capital or student achievement. The more effective principals were those who defined their role as *facilitators* of teacher success rather than instructional leaders. (Leana, 2011, p. 35, emphasis in original)

Let's not misinterpret the direction that these findings are taking us. The implication is not that principals should abandon the focus on instruction, but rather that they should get at it by working with teachers individually and collectively to develop *their* professional capital. The press for continuous instructional improvement is central. There is still a lot of precision to be had—what specific expertise is needed for learning in math, what teams are needed for what tasks, what the new pedagogy is that has students as partners in learning and uses technology to accelerate and deepen learning. The principal is in there by helping the group get that good. The question is what combination of factors will maximize that press for most teachers learning and therefore for most students learning.

Schools that invest in both human and social capital and make them interact build the resources required for schoolwide success. They quite simply come to have the wherewithal to accomplish wider and deeper results. The principal's role is to participate as a learner and leader in ensuring that the combined human and social capital forces are devoted to outcomes in a targeted, continuous manner. Further development on the job is the key. We know that most teachers do not get ongoing feedback about the quality of their teaching. The question, then, is what conditions or processes best serve that purpose. I have already observed that formal appraisal schemes represent a crude and ineffective method as the main mechanism for giving constructive feedback. How many professions do you know in which formal appraisal looms as the major instrument of improvement? There are better ways of improving all teachers or of getting rid of the bottom 5%, one of them being strong collaborative cultures (i.e., social capital). If you make culture the main strategy, formal feedback becomes a lot easier. Thus much of the effective feedback becomes built into the day-to-day purposeful interactions of the culture at work. And recall that the effective principal participates in shaping the culture of learning. It is more natural, organic, and by definition persistent so that it is more effective. Most teachers want constructive feedback to get better, and most find it lacking in the culture of the profession.

In my experience, formal appraisal schemes always become counterproductive when people bend over backward to separate coaching from evaluation, for example, by specifying that instructional coaches should give only non-evaluative feedback or by making principals responsible only for formal, consequential evaluation. This separation typically is associated with *low-trust cultures.* It's there to protect. But put all the protective mechanisms you want in a low-trust culture, and you will still never get motivated development. All feedback in a sense is evaluative, and when carried out *primarily for growth* it results in improvement. If feedback that is acted on is the main point, and surely it should be, then let's see how that can be accomplished best and not make formal appraisal an end in itself.

Systems can and should "get evaluation right" in the formal sense. The Organisation for Economic Co-operation and Development (OECD, 2013) has well summarized the key issues concerning using evaluation to improve teaching. Its TALIS survey of teachers in 25 countries strikes all-too-familiar notes: 22% of the teachers have never had any feedback from their principals (not to mention whether the feedback was valuable from any of those who did get appraised), over 50% have never received feedback from external source, yet 79% of teachers would find constructive feedback helpful. And as OECD also found, there are increasingly good formal appraisal frameworks around the world that contain valuable components and standards. The TALIS survey also found that 55% of teachers want more PD, but only if it is connected to their growth and implementation of improved practices. Only 33% report that they are engaged in cooperative professional learning communities, that is, collaborative cultures (Weatherby, 2013).

Formal teacher appraisal can never be the main driver of improving the profession. But since most jurisdictions are developing and requiring formal appraisal, let's position it effectively:

1. Make the appraisal framework sound (based on best standards and efficient ways of assessing them).
2. Underpin its use with a development/improvement philosophy versus an evaluative/punitive stance.
3. Make the learning culture of schools and districts the main event, and integrate any performance appraisal in the service of this shared work.
4. Ensure that professional development/learning is a fundamental ongoing feature of the entire process.
5. Realize that by far the most effective and telling feedback that teachers will get is what is built into the purposeful interaction between and among teachers and the principal. Such interaction is specific to the task of learning. For example, collective analysis of evidence of student learning and the practices that lead to greater learning is at the heart of continuous improvement.

In short, schools should use formal appraisal of human capital to buttress the work of day-to-day improvement, but should not expect it to have major impact on organizational learning. For the latter you need well-led groups working together to make specific changes in instruction tied to student learning.

As I suggested earlier, social capital is expressed in the interactions and relationships among the staff of any school that support a common cause. There is no question that a group with plenty of social culture is able to accomplish much more than a group with little—not a correlation, but cause and effect. Interpersonal trust and individual expertise work hand in hand toward better results. Social capital increases your knowledge because it gives you access to other people's human capital.

Absence of social capital helps explain why professional development often does not have much effect. Peter Cole (2004) was formerly with the Victoria (Australia) Department of Education and Training and is now a consultant who focuses on professional learning. Who could not be intrigued by the title of his article: "Professional Development: A Great Way to Avoid Change!" in which he describes how people go to workshops, feel as if they are learning something new, and rarely follow through. Of course, what matters is what happens after (or between) workshops: Who tries things out? Who supports you? Who gives you feedback? Who picks you up when you make a mistake? Who else can you learn from? How can you take responsibility for change together? Productive answers to all of these questions depend on the culture to which one returns, especially its social capital. Cole's (2013) paper *Aligning Professional Learning, Performance Management and Effective Teaching* draws similar conclusions to the case I am making here: Make the culture of the school and the district the main focus, not the qualifications or expertise of individual humans.

Both Bryk and Leithwood show that developing the social capital of schools and that of the community forms a powerful combination. When schools work on their own social capital, they are more likely to see parents and the community as part of the solution; when they remain isolated individualistic cultures, they can easily treat parents as part of the problem, thereby reinforcing a downward spiral.

As noted above, decisional capital refers to resources of knowledge, intelligence, and energy that are required to put human and social capital to effective use. It is basically the capacity to choose well and make good decisions. It is best thought of as expertise that grows over time. It should be thought of at both the individual (i.e., a given teacher's expertise) and group levels (i.e., the collective judgment of two or more teachers). Like decision making itself, the process of accumulating decisional capital should also be deliberate. In schools, principals must have great decisional capital of their own, but even more of it should reside in the many other individuals and groups of which schools are composed. When human and social capital merge over time, based on the expertise of the people learning through deliberate practice, their professional judgment becomes more powerful.

This decisional form of professional capital can easily be taken for granted, yet it is at the heart of any profession. Working in isolation does not usually increase this type of expertise. Nor does working together automatically increase it. Beware of schools where teachers appear to be working together but mainly run on contrived collegiality, where administrators have mandated professional learning communities (PLCs), or "cozy collaboration," in which there is little focus and intensity of effort.

Instead, decisional capital is developed through deep learning cultures. Consider an example from outside the field of education per se. When Liker and Meier (2007), who have studied Toyota over the years, found that Toyota's culture was so effective at continuous learning linked to top performance, they traced this strength to "the depth of understanding among Toyota's employees regarding their work" (p. 112). I prefer to say *shared depth.* You don't get depth at a workshop, you don't get it just by hiring great individuals, and you don't get it through congenial relationships. You develop shared depth through continuous learning, solving problems, and getting better and better at what you do. Developing expertise day after day by making learning and its impact the focus of the work is what pays off. Expertise, individual and collective, on a wide basis is what counts.

In schools and educational systems, decisional capital is about cultivating human and social capital over time, deliberately identifying and spreading the instructional practices that are most effective for the learning goals of the school. People don't learn these once and for all (and in some cases if at all) in preservice teacher education programs. They learn them best by practicing on the job, having access to coaches and skilled peers. In education, as in any profession, there are discretionary decisions to make to determine the most effective response to the situation at hand. When a parent puts a difficult question to a teacher who has to consult the manual or check the scripted lesson, you know that teacher is not a professional.

When the school is organized to focus on a small number of shared goals, and when professional learning is targeted to those goals and is a collective enterprise, the evidence is overwhelming that teachers can do dramatically better by way of student achievement. Well-led school-based learning with peers is the best way to learn the fundamentals of teaching—let's call them the nonnegotiable basics. When University of Melbourne education researcher John Hattie conducted his in-depth research analysis of over 1,000 meta-studies, he did us a favor by identifying the high-impact teaching practices. These practices (e.g., feedback to students, frequent examining and acting on effects of teaching, metacognition where students become self-aware and in control more of their own learning, peer learning among students) are best learned explicitly and with peers.

At the end of the day, says Hattie (2009), expert teachers "can provide defensible evidence of positive impacts of teaching on student learning." You get that way through deliberate practice on a continuous basis, which can be done on one's own, but is much more likely to occur if forcefully led and accelerated by the group. The latter is the only way to foster expertise at scale. If you want to change the group, use the group to change the group. The role of the principal in this endeavor is clear: It is to help establish challenging goals and corresponding environments "for teachers to critique, question, and support other teachers to reach these goals [that] have the most effect on student outcomes" (p. 83).

In one of his best sellers, *Outliers,* Malcolm Gladwell made the 10,000-hour rule famous. That figure comes up time and again for individuals trying to become accomplished at their trade: 10,000 hours of deliberate practice over 10 years or more. It is what separates professionals from the rest of us. I suppose it is obvious that this process can be accelerated when people are learning from each other, and that, equally, it may never succeed (except for the odd genius) if a person simply goes it alone. Teaching is not the kind of profession where staying cloistered will often result in one's achieving personal mastery or ending up having much collective impact.

So it is practice at exercising judgment and a great deal of it that accumulates decisional capital. And power of judgment is sharpened and accelerated when it is mediated through learning with colleagues (social capital). High-yield strategies become more precise and more embedded when they are developed and deployed in teams that are constantly refining and interpreting them according to impact on students across the school. At the same time, poor judgmental practices and ineffective procedures get discarded along the way. When clear evidence is lacking or conflicting, accumulated collective experience carries much more weight than idiosyncratic experience.

Expertise and judgment become all the more critical in time of innovation. The Common Core State Standards (CCSS) represents a potential powerful opportunity or a disaster of titanic proportions, depending on the decisional capital of the teaching force and school leaders. Now that standards and assessments are being spelled out, the difficulty will be how to develop the best learning in relation to the standards. Some states may very well provide specific directives that strip teachers of the opportunity to make independent judgments. Others may leave it to the discretion of individual teachers, with equally problematic results. In any case I think it is accurate to say that, at this stage of the evolution of CCSS, standards are the strongest part of the new direction, assessment is the second strongest, and by far the weakest is curriculum and instruction (or, if you like, pedagogy). This underscores my main conclusion that collaborative cultures focusing on instructional practice are a crucial part of implementing LF's implementation standard.

In this section I have examined school cultures and included the role of the principal. It is also the case that these same principles apply when learning is teacher led. The Teacher Learning and Leadership Program in Ontario is a case in point. Jointly developed by the Ontario Teachers' Federation (the umbrella union for teachers) and the Ontario Ministry of Education, this program provides grants to two or more teachers who pursue learning and implementation relative to proposed topics (Campbell, Lieberman, & Yashkina, 2013). Typical topics are differentiated instruction, literacy, technology, and professional learning communities. In all these cases learning in the context in which you are working (i.e., learning through implementation) is featured. The evaluators found that the vast majority of teachers were satisfied with the experience and implemented ideas together.

School District Level

It has become increasingly clear that district cultures make a huge difference with respect to the LF implementation standard. In the same way that isolated teachers don't learn as well, isolated schools do not learn as much as they should *even if they are collaborative within their walls.* I won't spend as much time discussing the details in this section as I did in the previous ones, because the main argument has been well set. I have also documented the success of whole districts in other publications. In *All Systems Go* (Fullan, 2010), I furnish profiles of Tower Hamlets in London, England, Long Beach Unified in California, and York Region and Ottawa Catholic in Ontario. And in *Moral Imperative Realized* (Fullan, 2011), I profile Sanger District in California and Fort Bend in Texas. All these districts, ranging in size from 15 to 190 schools, exemplify districtwide learning cultures in which ongoing professional learning is central to their success as measured by significant gains in student achievement over periods of 10 years or more. This theme is further taken up in a publication focusing on broadening the role of the principalship (Fullan, 2014).

In effect, I am saying that for the LF standard to be best implemented, we must focus on changing the culture of districts, which of course means changing the culture of schools and their relationships. We have helped implement and have studied these developments. They revolve around altering two dimensions in concert: One concerns vertical relationships between the district and the schools toward a focused two-way partnership; the second and related involves horizontal learning relationships across schools where clusters of schools learn from each other. The effect of these two dimensions intersecting is that purposeful learning is greatly enhanced. Much of this work is focused and specific: how to improve literacy, what works best for math, how data are used to link assessment and instruction, who is getting good results, and so on. The outcome is greater mutual allegiance, where people begin to identify with and support each other with the performance of the system being mutually valued, and greater collaborative competition, where people try to outdo themselves and each other for the good of the system. In all of these cases, the performance of the system substantially improves, and greater sustainability becomes evident.

All of this is corroborated in the extensive work that Rick DuFour and his colleagues have carried out with respect to professional learning communities. DuFour and I name several examples at the school and district levels of well-implemented PLCs where professional learning and student achievement are systemic across all classrooms and schools in the district (DuFour & Fullan, 2013). This work is tantamount to implementing changes in culture that were depicted in Figure 1.1.

In short, implementation of the professional learning standard is best served when the district as a whole, and all of its schools, are engaged in a multifaceted partnership to create conditions favorable to ongoing learning and increased performance for all—adults and students alike.

System Level

At the system level there is one set of policies that are necessary but not sufficient for professional learning. These polices pertain to professional standards for teacher preparation and for the teaching profession. They also involve teacher appraisal and evaluation. Two good sources that capture the key issues and directions are Linda Darling-Hammond (2013) and OECD (2013). I called these necessary but insufficient, so let me explain. Standards and practices for appraisal frame the problem in a good way, but there are two major reasons that they are not sufficient to implement the LF standard. One is that standards inevitably end up focusing on human capital (e.g., attracting, retaining, and developing better teachers). This is useful, but systems can never be substantially changed by relying solely on individuals. As I made clear in the previous two sections, you must also employ collective strategies that foster individuals and groups learning from each other in a purposeful, specific manner. What does this look like at the system level?

Keeping with the theme of this chapter, what we need are polices and strategies whereby learning within the big system—regions, states, provinces, countries—is deliberately promoted. We always like to be specific about the nature of this work, what actually happens, and what impact it might have on teacher learning and student achievement. The goal is to enable big systems to achieve greater coherence as it relates to performance. One strategy that we are currently engaged in in California is what we call *leading from the middle* (with the middle defined as districts). One can think of three levels—local schools and communities, districts, and systems as a whole.

Leadership from the middle means a combination of several elements occurring simultaneously:

1. Districts get their own internal house in order as learning cultures.
2. Districts form collaboratives whereby they learn from each other.
3. Districts thus become better partners for working with the state, the unions, and others.

We are currently engaged in one major endeavor along these lines, which, if it works, will be a prize example because of its complexity. I am referring to the state of California. As educators in the state work to achieve greater coherence, the key stakeholders have invited our team to join the strategy. California is big and complex—40 million people, 7 million students, some 18,000 schools, and over 1,000 districts. It has been in decline for the past 30 years in budgetary and performance terms. But it always had great pockets of innovation and success. And now it has new money, new leadership, and widespread groups who want to engage in new partnerships to reverse its 30-year trend of decline. Some of the key players are the governor, the state board, the state superintendent and California Department of Education, the Association of California School Administrators, and the California Teachers Association.

It is too early to determine success, but let's use a concrete illustration. One collaborative of districts is called the California Office of Reform in Education (CORE), a name left over from a failed Race to the Top proposal. CORE consists of 10 districts that represent some 20% of the students in California. It has its own board, executive director, and staff. One of its first strategies (beautifully tied to the theme of this chapter) is to use the expertise in the 10 districts to help develop struggling schools. The design is that X number of schools in difficulty will be paired with Y number of more successful schools with similar demographics, and they will be given some resources and support—all with a view toward helping to develop the schools. All of this is to happen in a nonjudgmental atmosphere (a key condition in our change theory for whole-system change). We can predict that the so-called helpers will learn as much as the helpees.

CORE is inviting other districts to join. We are also exploring establishing other district collaboratives in the state (in fact, there are some in existence). The idea is to mobilize the capacity and focus of all districts to help each other in deep implementation and to become better proactive partners with the state, unions, and others. The whole process is complex but not so hard to grasp. My point is, as with everything that I have said in this chapter, for success we must increase the intensity and frequency of learning on an ongoing basis. At the system level it will be the combination of good standards and polices *and* changes in the cultures of schools, districts, and the state that will ultimately be required for success.

A recent review of change strategies in my book *The Principal: Three Keys for Maximizing Impact* (Fullan, 2014) has confirmed the gist of the findings pertaining to the implementation standard. The principal must focus on leading learning, not on micromanaging instruction or on managerial work only; needs to be a system player participating in networks with other schools and in related district-wide reform; and must be a great change agent who can move the school forward under difficult circumstances.

In conclusion, the main argument in this chapter has deep meaning. Reflect on Learning Forward's implementation standard one more time:

> Implementation: Professional learning that increases educator effectiveness and results for all students applies research on change and sustains support for implementation of professional learning for long-term change.

We have seen that implementing this implementation standard will require changes in the culture of the entire system. These changes are not abstract and can be readily identified as I have done. They leverage best practices across the system. Such practices are continuously grounded on and tested against evidence of impact. There is thus limited formal distinction between effective practice and research. Finally, I hope the point of the chapter is not lost that because professional learning is embedded in changing culture, *sustainability is built in!*

References

Borman, K. M., and Associates. (2005). *Meaningful urban education reform.* Albany: State University of New York Press.

Bryk, A., Bender-Sebring, P., Allensworth, E., Luppescu, S., & Easton, J. (2010). *Organizing for school improvement: Lessons from Chicago.* Chicago, IL: University of Chicago Press.

Campbell, C., Lieberman, A., & Yashkina, A. (2013). *Teacher learning and leadership program.* Toronto, Ontario, Canada: Ontario Ministry of Education, Ontario Teachers Federation.

Cohen, D., & Hill, H. (2001). *Learning policy.* New Haven, CT: Yale University Press.

Cole, P. (2004). *Professional development: A great way to avoid change* (Seminar Series 194). Melbourne, Australia: Centre for Strategic Education.

Cole, P. (2013). *Aligning professional learning, performance management and effective teaching* (Seminar Series 217). Melbourne, Australia: Centre for Strategic Education.

Cross City Campaign for Urban School Reform. (2005). *A delicate balance: District policies and classroom practice.* Chicago, IL: Author.

Cuban, L. (2013). *Inside the black box of classroom practice.* Cambridge, MA: Harvard Education Press.

Darling-Hammond, L. (2013). *Getting teacher evaluation right.* New York, NY: Teachers College Press.

DuFour, R., & Fullan, M. (2013). *Built to last: Making PLCs systemic.* Bloomington, IN: Solution Tree.

Fullan, M. (2007). *The new meaning of educational change* (4th ed.). New York, NY: Teachers College Press.

Fullan, M. (2010). *All systems go: The change imperative for whole system reform.* Thousand Oaks, CA: Corwin.

Fullan, M. (2011). *The moral imperative realized.* Thousand Oaks, CA: Corwin.

Fullan, M. (2013). *Stratosphere: Integrating technology, pedagogy, and change knowledge.* Toronto, Ontario, Canada: Pearson.

Fullan, M. (2014). *The principalship: Three keys for maximizing impact.* San Francisco, CA: Jossey-Bass.

Fullan, M., Hill, P., & Crevola, C. (2006). *Breakthrough.* Thousand Oaks, CA: Corwin.

Fullan, M., & Pomfret, A. (1977). Research on curriculum and instruction implementation. *Review of Educational Research,* 47, 335–397.

Gladwell, M. (2008). *Outliers: The story of success.* New York, NY: Little, Brown.

Goodlad, J. I., Klein, M. F., & Associates. (1970). *Behind the classroom door.* Worthington, OH: Charles Jones.

Gross, N., Giacquinta, J., & Bernstein, M. (1971). *Implementing organizational innovations.* New York, NY: Basic Books.

Hargreaves, A., & Fullan, M. (2013). *Professional capital: Transforming teaching in every school.* New York, NY: Teachers College Press.

Hattie, J. (2009). *Visible learning.* London, UK: Routledge.

Leana, C. (2011). The missing link in school reform. *Stanford Social Innovation Review, 9*(4).

Leithwood, K. (2011). *Characteristics of high performing school districts in Ontario.* Toronto, Ontario, Canada: OISE/University of Toronto.

Liker, J., & Meier, D. (2007). *Toyota talent.* New York, NY: McGraw-Hill.

Organisation for Economic Co-operation and Development. (2013). *Teachers for the 21st Century: Using evaluation to improve teaching.* Paris, France: Author.

Robinson, V. (2011). *Student-centered leadership.* San Francisco, CA: Jossey-Bass.

Sarason, S. (1971). *The culture of the school and the problem of change.* Boston, MA: Allyn & Bacon.

Timperley, H. (2011). *Realizing the power of professional learning.* New York, NY: McGraw-Hill.

Weatherby, K. (2013). *A class act: Giving teachers feedback.* Paris, France: OECDToday.

Chapter Two

Implementation—Where Art Thou?

Shirley M. Hord

Here is a river flowing now very fast.
It is so great and swift that there are those
who will be afraid, who will try to hold on to the shore.

The time for the lone wolf is over.
Gather yourselves.

All that we do now must be done
in a sacred manner and in celebration.
For we are the ones we have been waiting for.

—from the Elders of the Hopi Nation

Associate Superintendent Glen Linsang and Director of Professional Development and Curriculum and Instruction Gail Johnson met with the middle school's Mathematics Department chair, Marcia Washington, and its principal, Jonathan Lopez, at the end of the school day in the (now vacated) teachers' lounge. All appeared restless and dispirited as PD Director Gail said, "Our mathematics pilot teachers are not using the new math instructional approach nor its content. After all that we've done to prepare for this transition, it just isn't happening. Are the teachers afraid of this approach, or are they just stubborn? What's going on here?"

Associate Superintendent Glen reviewed the actions that had already been taken by the district: "Each member of the superintendent's cabinet, and the entire school board, is on board and in support of the new program. We all agree that this is our big chance to address our students' needs and to demonstrate to our parents and community that we are doing just that. Each of us in the district office is committed to this new approach, and we've demonstrated this commitment by investing time, resources, professional development—whatever is needed. We even brought in national experts to help us better understand the new mathematics curriculum."

Principal Jon shared, "It's all true, and you should know how much we appreciate the district's generosity. We've responded by taking specific actions at our school to support the new program. We gave the teachers a new schedule so that they can teach the pilot math classes at the beginning of the day when everyone is fresh."

"I've checked to make certain that every teacher has all the materials and resources necessary to succeed with this innovative program," added Department Chair Marcia. "And I've checked to see that teachers have the daily assignments in their lesson plans, but we are stymied."

"Absolutely!" added Jon. "Here in the school, we've emphasized it in grade-level meetings, and we told parents about it in our back-to-school night at the beginning of the school year nearly a year ago. Do you remember, we even held a make-your-own super sundae event for the students in the pilot to get them focused on a new approach to learning math. I don't know what's happening, but one thing I know for sure is that what we've been doing isn't working. Our interim assessments have been telling us that for several months."

"I'm so disappointed," Marcia said. "I'm convinced that this new approach is what our students need, across the district, to prepare them for college and 21st century careers. They need to develop a new understanding of how mathematics works, but more than that, new insights into the relationships of various mathematical computations, like how multiplication relates to division. Why aren't they getting on board? Why isn't it sticking?" Her voice trailed off.

Dear reader, have you, too, been at this place?

An Urgent Problem— But Unfortunately So Typical

To *improve* any human endeavor, whether it is producing a luscious cherry-apricot cobbler or a more effective approach to teaching phonics, we must *change* what is not effective to something that promises increased success. And in order to accomplish this, we must *learn* what the change is and how to use it.

Clearly, then, improvement is based on change, which is based on learning. The process of this learning and change is *implementation.* The success of implementation is dependent on learning that is of the highest quality and grounded in standards for its conduct. For this reason the application of all seven of Learning Forward's standards for professional learning, most explicitly the standard of implementation (cited at the beginning of this book), is essential to any school improvement effort.

A brief history of these standards, as well as a short narrative of the evolution of attention to implementation, is useful to our understanding.

Standards for Professional Learning

In 1995 Learning Forward (then named National Staff Development Council; NSDC) published 22 standards to guide the planning and conduct of (then called) staff development. These standards had been created by representatives of all organizations, associations, and agencies invested and/or interested in the continuous learning and development, and increasing effectiveness, of educators. Three editions of these standards addressed elementary, middle, and high schools.

After several years of efforts to promote the use of these standards, the executive director of NSDC called me to lament, "They're not using them!"

Addressing this assessment, the conversation turned to the large number of standards and the possible need to revise the number and content. This was done in 2001, when 12 standards were identified. A year later, my phone rang again, with the same message: They're not using them!

Interestingly, this international educational organization was experiencing the same implementation problems as those experienced by the district and middle school featured in the example that opened this chapter.

After sympathizing and problem exploring, we shifted the conversation to what to do. At this point, Stephanie Hirsh, the executive director, said, "I think that we need to create Innovation Configuration maps [a component of a research-based approach to change management—the Concerns-Based Adoption Model] that will provide word pictures of the standards in practice. For our constituents don't understand what these new practices are or what they should look like in action." She nailed it!

Two years was allocated to the creation of Innovation Configuration (IC) maps for the 12 standards and 11 educator roles (principal, teacher, central office staff, etc.), published in 2003. Persons related to and responsible for professional development (the nomenclature has changed from staff development) expressed a significant appreciation for these maps. After a positive response to the initial set of maps, the subsequent revision of Standards for Professional Learning (published in 2011) was followed by three volumes of maps for school-based roles, school system roles, and external providers. Fundamentally, the adoption of the IC concept and maps by Learning Forward represented the initiation of the ongoing partnership between professional learning and the art and science of change management. This makes excellent sense, for as noted, change is based on learning, and the purpose of learning is to support change.

The Attention to Implementation

Implementation is a critical part of the process of school change and improvement, but as Michael Fullan mentioned in the previous chapter, it has traditionally been the "black box" of the school improvement process (Cuban, 2013). This, despite the action of the U.S. Department of Education that has funded significant efforts to unveil and give support and direction to implementation of new classroom practice (and other innovations) that would benefit the successful learning of all students.

We know and understand that any change is grounded in *learning* what that change is and how to use it. We know that deleting nonproductive programs or practices in exchange for new, potentially productive ones (i.e., changing) is the basis for *improvement* of practice.

The success of the *Sputnik* launch by the former Soviet Union in the late 1950s led to widespread criticism of our public schools for failing to adequately prepare K–12 students in the areas of math and science. The public's outcry led school districts to bring on board numerous science and math curricula, but at the end of the year, student evaluation reports claimed no progress. Thus, the reigning curricula were dropped and new ones brought in. This annual cycle of adopt, evaluate, and discontinue the curriculum held sway until a group of wise individuals hypothesized that perhaps it wasn't the programs at fault, but possibly the process used to implement these programs was not sufficient.

To this end, the U.S. Department of Education funded a research program that would uncover and promote understanding of the essentials for implementation.

Implementation Research

Enter the research team and its rigorous agenda at the Research & Development Center for Teacher Education (R&D Center), University of Texas–Austin, which vigorously studied this issue in schools, districts, and colleges across the nation for more than a decade. The research continues, but under the guidance of individuals, globally. The research results were significant and are known as the Concerns-Based Adoption Model (CBAM).

Although there are certainly other references that direct attention to questions of implementation, the CBAM is a proven, research-based approach to changing initiation and implementation that has been successfully used for several decades to ensure that any new approach, initiative, or endeavor (however the change is characterized) will be found in its intended setting and remain for its intended duration. While the CBAM is used in the corporate sector, the military, and other environments, this suite of concepts/constructs, tools, and strategies was explicitly studied and tested for application to the education context.

There are two major divisions of the CBAM:

- a set of strategies, or actions, required for successful implementation and change
- a kit of tools that provides diagnostic information to the implementers of the change that is used to adjust or modify the strategies for their greatest effect

Strategies as a Frame for Implementation Action

Six research-based implementation strategies (Hord & Roussin, 2013) have resulted from the longitudinal research program of the

CBAM. This section elaborates on each of these strategies and their significance to implementation. But before the focus on implementation, a very brief reminder about the adoption process that brought the new program into the school.

Why introduce a new program or practice into the classrooms of a school or across all schools in a district? Such an action should not be taken without a clearly articulated basis for why it should be incorporated into the life of the school or district. Most schools with wise leadership at the helm use an improvement process with the staff to guide the identification and adoption of new practice that promises to improve staff effectiveness and, subsequently, students' successful learning. A very brief description of the steps of this adoption process calls attention to

- the study of multiple forms and sources of data to reveal areas of students' high and low performance and, if several areas are in need of attention (not unusual), the determination of which area to give preference for immediate attention;
- the use of educator and system data to uncover factors that impact the teaching/learning process in schools;
- the search for and decision to adopt potential new practices or a program—a change that the school or district will use to replace what is currently producing low performance, based on the data study noted above.

Deciding on and adopting a new practice, even with the fanfare typically accompanying its announcement, does not ensure the new practice will find its way into classrooms where it can benefit students' learning. Implementation is the key, and we now turn to six actions that support and guide implementation.

Strategy 1—Create a Shared Vision of the Change When It Has Been Integrated Into Practice in a High-Quality Way

If one considers an automobile trip as a metaphor for the journey of a new program or practice implementation, it becomes abundantly clear that the destination or designated end point must be established. And the end point must be clearly noted so that arrival can be assessed—and celebrated. Thus, the first step in moving toward a future of improved educational practice is the creation of a vision, or mental image, of what the new practice will look like when it is implemented in a high-quality way. This vision is vital so that all who are involved will be en route to the same end point, or result, that contributes meaningfully to increased student learning. It is anticipated that increased student outcomes will result from the specific innovation, or change, selected for adoption and implementation—if it has been an appropriate and wise selection.

Many change initiatives fail because implementers do not have clarity about what the new program is or how to use it. See three teachers' very different pictures of a new program, reported in the Innovation Configurations section later in the chapter. Recall also from earlier in the chapter the example of Learning Forward's executive director engaging the use of Innovation Configuration maps to clarify and create mental pictures of the Standards for Professional Learning so that educators might fully understand what high-quality professional learning would look like in practice in schools and districts. This vision or mental image of the change is more than the pronouncement of a lofty goal(s). It is written text that defines the specifics of the vision so that detailed precision is gained.

How is this vision of the innovation clarified and shared so that all constituents are on the same page? A major reason for the construct of IC maps was to serve this purpose, as noted earlier in this chapter. The map's purpose is to portray the innovation in action, wherever it is to be used. It describes best practices with the innovation and articulates less desirable practices expected as the novice user of the new program is learning about it and about how to become expert in implementing it.

The vision of the change must be tirelessly communicated so that everyone is continuously moving in step toward the same outcome. The communication may be delivered by principals, lead teachers, and other facilitators and supporters of the change. The communication may be distributed by printed school and district newsletters, through electronic media, at community meetings such as those of the town council or school board, in the checkout line in the local grocery store, and on the golf course. In short, wherever educators and their constituents gather, all are reminded of the school's vision, the rationale for the vision, and reports on progress in realizing the vision.

The creation and communication of a shared vision of the change, vis-à-vis an IC map, describes what educators will be doing in the workplace in terms of the new practice. This shared vision, communicated by the map, is exceptionally valuable as it can be applied to serve several of the strategies for implementing the change.

Strategy 2—Invest in Professional Learning

This text has consistently maintained that no change can succeed without effective learning about the change. Thus, the use of the term *invest* for this strategy is valid and speaks to the significance of effective, standards-based professional learning for educators in our schools and colleges.

The source of what is to be learned is found in the IC map that is noted in Strategy 1. This map informs the change leader and the implementer concretely through action words—what the implementer will be doing when implementation has been successful. Therefore, the IC map communicates what the change is, while the Standards for Professional Learning articulate the qualities, characteristics, and conditions for the professional learning that will result in implementation of the change.

These learning opportunities should be provided on an ongoing schedule as novice implementers develop expertise in using the new practice. All too often, professional learning is provided solely as a 2-day session at the beginning of the school year, instead of shorter sessions at periodic intervals and when the participants have had the chance to implement the previous learning. In addition to using the IC map as a guide to implementation learning, the Stages of Concern can be used to gain insight into implementers' concerns and needs in order to tailor the content and process of the learning events. This concept and its measures are described in the Tools and Techniques That Support Implementation section later in the chapter.

Change leaders must be deeply knowledgeable about the content and skillful in the processes for supporting the learning of the implementers. They must also be cognizant of developing implementers' positive attitudes about using new practices. They need to model and demonstrate use of the innovation for the adult learners as well as clarify misconceptions about the new program.

There is widespread acceptance of the idea that telling adult learners about a new practice or supplying text about it will be sufficient for their learning. Research on both effective staff development/ professional learning and change processes indicate that several stages are necessary to enable learners of new practices to transfer their learning to classrooms, or whatever the intended setting may be. The research of Joyce and Showers (2002, pp. 78–79) is clearly and succinctly instructive about what is needed for learners to be able to learn and put the learning into place in classrooms (see Figure 2.1). They report three outcomes (knowledge, skill, transfer) and four components of training, or professional learning (study of theory, demonstration, practice, peer coaching).

What is easily seen in Figure 2.1 is that the study of theory (telling or reading about a new practice) provides no accomplishment for transfer (executive implementation) of the practice into the classroom. Nor does demonstration add to this accomplishment. While practice (with feedback) makes a significant increase in knowledge and skills, there is a scant 5% success in transferring into the work setting.

What makes the significant difference in all outcomes (knowledge, skill, transfer) is the cumulative use of the first three components, and the addition of peer coaching, that has been the focus of attention by these researchers for significant years and in multiple settings.

Figure 2.1 Training Components and Attainment of Outcomes (% of Participants)

	Outcomes		
Components	*Knowledge (thorough)*	*Skill (strong)*	*Transfer (executive implementation)*
Study of Theory	10	5	0
Demonstration	30	20	0
Practice	60	60	5
Peer Coaching	95	95	95

Source: Joyce & Showers, 2002. Used with permission.

Thus, if implementation—that is, transfer into practice—is to be reached, the implementer's learning must be designed to include all four of these learning activities/supports.

For change leaders planning for successful implementation, this means investing significant time for the learning and significant stretches of time—even years—for the transfer of the learning, as well as providing competent coaches. In addition, there must be the consideration of a well-conceived and clearly articulated plan to guide these activities and to identify resources needed for the success of the plan, to which we next turn.

Strategy 3—Plan for Implementation and Identify the Required Resources

A well-articulated vision is of no value unless there are clear directions to guide the grade-level team, the school, the district, or the state department of education in realizing the vision. Hence, a plan for implementing the vision is vital. This plan provides clear, explicit, and orderly steps for reaching implementation. The collaborative, and wise, leader engages the staff in constructing the plan and in the conversation about resources needed and their effective use.

Budgets may require the careful scrutiny of line items and their monetary allocation. Staff members may be required to take on roles different from their current assignment. Involving staff in conversations about these issues and how best to use staff, time, and fiscal resources can lead to understanding if or when hard-to-accept decisions about resources must be taken. Collaboration and transparency, again, should rule the conversation about planning implementation and the related resource needs.

Although a plan must be specific and clear, planning is not cast in concrete, nor is it a one-time event. As the process of implementation progresses, there may well be the need to adapt the plan to accommodate for what is working successfully and what is not. Effective leaders interact with the staff and work with them in making these adjustments in allocations for time, energy, personnel, and dollars. Although it would seem abundantly clear, there are some implementation planners who ignore the vital need for appropriate resources that allow and support implementers to initiate, adjust, and sustain implementation. Implementation efforts without sufficient material and human resources (such as support personnel) may lead to delays and frustrations or may even be doomed from the outset. (This topic is explored in depth in the *Resources* volume of this series.)

Resources may be reallocated more than once, although certainly such adjustments should be minimized. These adjustments are used to maximize educators' professional learning and its implementation and subsequently lead to students' improved learning.

In considering the allocation of resources, one wise rule of thumb when planning implementation of new practice is to use "prioritized abandonment," according to Larry Lezotte. The concept here is to consider the array of programs or practices that inevitably land on educators' plates for implementation. Rarely can all of them be given sufficient attention and resources simultaneously for successful implementation. Thus, the idea is to identify what is the most compelling . . . and trash the rest.

In a slightly different way, Jim Collins (2001), in *Good to Great,* suggests maintaining focus and disallowing distractions to interfere. Along with attention to resource allocation and logistical factors, implications of state and district policies and their changes impact implementation, so beware of taking too many possibilities on board simultaneously.

Professional learning is a significant part of the plan. Successful change leaders always have their eye on the vision and its realization, understanding that the Standards for Professional Learning provide a starting point through which the staff experiences, learns, and gains expertise.

Strategy 4—Monitor Progress

In this strategy, change facilitators will be investigating each implementer's implementation status by exploring his or her growth and progress as he or she engages in the learning, practice, and feedback. The idea is to monitor the status of implementation of the vision, but to do so in a supportive manner and to share feedback with the implementer in order to achieve more complete implementation.

The words *evaluation, monitor,* and *assess* clearly suggest comparison to a goal (in this case the vision) and also hold the probability of negative reactions by the implementer, especially if that individual is being strongly challenged to put the vision into operation. Therefore, a word of caution about language—the "exploring growth" label seems very appropriate, and more acceptable to novices.

It is at this point in the implementation game plan that action so frequently breaks down. Unless change facilitators or coaches are well prepared for the one-on-one monitoring interaction, with the knowledge and skills to conduct conversations about the individual's work with the innovation as prescribed by the vision, unfortunate feelings can develop. The development of trust is imperative, and, of course, this development should have been initiated long before the monitoring stage. Tschannen-Moran's (2004) work is especially useful here, for she has identified and described the qualities that change leaders and facilitators must have in order to develop trust in implementers. She notes these qualities:

- Benevolence—caring, extending goodwill, supporting others, expressing appreciation for efforts
- Honesty—telling the truth, keeping promises, honoring agreements
- Openness—engaging in open conversation, delegating, sharing information and decision making and power
- Reliability—being consistent and dependable, demonstrating commitment and diligence
- Competence—setting standards, pushing for results, setting an example, resolving conflict rather than avoidance, being flexible

In addition to these qualities, the facilitator/coach requires tools to aid in the conversation about progress so that explicit information is obtained. Once again, the IC map that portrays the vision is a powerful tool to use for guiding this conversation about progress. Further, this page of text can be referred to as the coach and the implementer collaboratively determine where on the horizontal continua of the variations the implementer "resides." The facilitator should always cross-check her or his identification of where the implementer falls on various continua with that of the implementer so that discrepancies or differences of opinion are resolved.

If a rating by the implementer seems off target, asking for an example of the action may be a good way to enlighten or resolve cloudy or disparate responses. If the implementer seems uncomfortable, engaging in the very brief, one-legged Stages of Concern interview (described in the Tools section) to discover reactions or feelings may be very useful to the facilitator in understanding the participant more fully.

A last thought is offered for consideration. It seems to express a degree of collegiality if the facilitator meets the implementer in the hallway and they proceed to the location for their conversation together, while engaging in casual or "idle" interchange about the snowfall last night, the school's football team possibilities, or such. If it is possible to sit at a round table, rather than the facilitator behind his or her desk, do it—again, to generate a feeling of collegiality. And be up front; provide a simple reason for taking any notes, such as because of the facilitator's faulty memory. Taking notes without any explanation can easily lead to suspicions by the implementer.

Strategy 5—Provide Ongoing Assistance

This strategy is tightly tied to Strategy 4, for assistance is not given frivolously and without clear intention. The information from Strategy 4 provides the basis for determining the support and assistance to be offered to the implementer. Having said that using words like *assess* may not be a good idea, the hand-in-glove alliteration of *assess and assist* reveals this relationship between Strategies 4 and 5. Appropriate assistance (Strategy 5) cannot be given without specific assessment of the implementer's progress (Strategy 4). This assessing and assisting work seems essentially to describe the work of coaches.

The assessing and assisting is where "the rubber meets the road," for this action duet results in identifying successes (and celebrating them, whether large or small) and identifying and providing support for whatever areas/factors need attention. For this activity, the facilitator must be skillful in sharing feedback—some would recommend sharing "warm" feedback initially, then "cool." Others have suggested that three "glows" should precede one "grow."

All of this is to say that much sensitivity and thoughtful reflection must take place to successfully help implementers at whatever state of progress they project.

But to repeat: Use tools or processes that will reveal clearly the status of the implementer's progress. Without accurate and authentic data, assistance cannot be on target, and implementation suffers. In addition, developing an inventory of useful and appropriate assistance actions that are attuned to the variety of implementers and their specific needs will be the facilitator's challenge.

Strategy 6—Create a Context Conducive to Change

It is important here to stress that while there is a logic to the sequence of these strategies, after their introduction all continue to be used throughout implementation. In contrast, the climate/context/culture conducive to conducting change strategy may be envisioned as an umbrella over all and in place before the initiation of an effort to implement a change. Having such a culture in place from the get-go is a definite "plus" factor for implementation; however, if such a culture does not exist, then this strategy must be given attention simultaneously with the introduction of the change vision and the IC map that describes it. Such a productive and positive culture then may be developed along with the implementation effort, but it will require additional attention, care, and action.

As has been consistently stated, school improvement or reform is dependent on the school staff changing how they operate in their classrooms and across the school. This change is dependent on the staff learning how to do things differently. Such change flourishes in a setting where everyone is committed to learning—learning by the staff first, followed by learning by the students.

Students become more effective learners when they are taught by continuously learning teachers and administrators. In such a setting, change is promoted and risk-taking encouraged. If mistakes are made by the adult learners, they are seen as opportunities for correction and learning. In this context, mistakes are not seen as traumatic but as part of the process of changing the school so that students benefit. As they begin to operate differently, staff may lack confidence. Thus, leaders give attention to the concerns of teachers and are never too busy to hear their needs for more information, help with materials and lesson preparation, assistance with new instructional strategies, and so on.

In a school that fosters a context conducive to change, all teachers and administrators come together periodically to reflect on whether and how they are achieving their goals for students. They identify what is working well and what is not. From reflecting and assessing, they determine what needs further attention and the learning in which they themselves need to engage.

Collaborative leaders engage in professional learning *with* teachers in order to support teachers in making changes in curriculum, instruction, assessment, and other areas. In this increasingly collegial environment, they encourage teachers to take leadership roles, and with teachers they share power, authority, and decision making. In this way, the entire school acts as a community of leaders and learners.

It should also be quite obvious that trust between and among staff, and between and among students, and between staff and students is a prerequisite to all the above.

Next, we discuss the tools that can be used to guide the strategies as well as suggestions for their use.

Tools and Techniques That Support Implementation

Three concepts and their measuring processes have been identified through long-term research and continuing practice. All three have been abundantly used in research and evaluation studies—and for their practical application in facilitating the implementation of change successfully. They are highly recommended for application to the six strategies and for guiding the implementer on his or her journey of change. The IC map has been noted a number of times in this chapter, and we discuss this construct and its tool as the first of the three concepts.

Innovation Configurations

As staff members were in the field verifying the theory and measures of earlier work on Levels of Use (LoU), almost immediately apparent was the need for the construct of Innovation Configurations (Hord, Stiegelbauer, Hall, & George, 2006).

A Challenging Problem. It is not difficult to recall, or imagine, this situation in a school that was focused on implementing a new mathematics curriculum.

In a third-grade classroom of an elementary school, the change researcher asked the teacher to describe the new mathematics curriculum that the school had adopted.

"Well," she said, "I wish I could really know what the curriculum is. I am confused about it, especially when chatting about it with my teacher neighbors on the third-grade wing. We would really like to be doing it *right,* but we don't know what right really is. We are all working with it in very different ways."

Another third-grade teacher, in response to the researcher's query, said, "I have a set of objectives sent by the district that guides me in my teaching math. I use the district-adopted math textbook and the district's supplemental kit, provided because all the objectives aren't included in the textbook. When I have completed a unit and its objective, I administer the district's assessment. When I receive the scores on that test, I move those students who passed on to the next objective, but for those who didn't meet the passing score, I reteach those students with alternate materials that I have created. Is that what you are interested in hearing about?"

In a third classroom, the teacher reported that she had been teaching third-grade math for a dozen years and knew what students needed to know: "I have a list of the objectives for the year. Would you like to see that? And I have activities and worksheets that I have accumulated over the years. I use a test that I have designed to ascertain whether students have achieved the objectives. Then we move on to the next unit and its objective. It would be fine if you want to visit the students in my classroom."

A fourth classroom teacher on the third grade wing described his math sessions: "I follow the textbook that was selected because it most closely follows the math curriculum that the district math coordinator adopted for us. Each chapter focuses on an objective, with a large number of practice problems for the students. I use the end-of-chapter tests to check students' accomplishments, then move to the next chapter. It works very efficiently, I think."

What to do? There were so many different iterations of the presumably same curricular program. And this school's circumstances were not new to the researchers, for they were hearing similar messages from a wide array of schools and districts. What appeared to be happening was that the new program was changing some teachers' practices, while some of the teachers were changing the program's practices. Through reflection, consideration, much discussion, and sometimes rather energetic debate among the researchers, these ruminations gave birth to the construct named Innovation Configurations.

Despite the provision of materials and professional development to teachers, principals, and others expected to implement new practices, these people very frequently are not clear about what to do. This results in a big gap between what is expected in classrooms and what is actually found there. Regardless of the origin of the change (local teachers or administrators, central office supervisors, regional agencies, state policymakers, or national experts), providing an explicit picture of what high quality-implementation looks like is imperative. To portray this vision of the innovation, the research team created the Innovation Configuration map. This instrument captures in writing the mental image of successful implementation of the innovation in action in the classroom or whatever its intended setting may be.

The IC Map. The map is arranged as a chart (see Figure 2.2), such that the components of the new program, practice, or process (that is, major pieces or parts, such as objectives, materials, instructional approaches, and assessment tools of an academic curriculum) are situated vertically and labeled Component 1, 2, 3, and so on. There are five components on this map. It is critical that each of these components be stated in action terms (verbs that are observable). Note in the upper left corner the term *teacher.* This identifies the role of the person for whom the IC map has been constructed. When *teacher* is placed in front of each of the component statements, a complete sentence can be created. For example: *Teacher selects objectives.* These indicate the components *in operation* in the intended setting.

For each component, the ideal variation is described in cell (1). Across the continuum, there is an array of variations decreasing in value from the ideal description of the component in cell (1). Note that there are not the same number of variations for all components. The variations are derived from predicting how teachers will be using the New Math Program (in the figure) and arranging them in decreasing value.

Measuring IC. As a result of a collaborative conversation with the facilitator that leads to the implementer's reflection, or an observation by a coach or other facilitator focused on the implementer using the innovation, one cell for each component can be marked that best reflects how the implementer is operating with the innovation. This instrument is meant to be a "growth-inducing" tool. Thus, it is important to mark as accurately as possible and in a collaborative mode, with the change facilitator and the implementer studying the descriptions and matching them to the implementer's current practice.

So that the descriptive cells can be marked as easily as possible, it is important not to put too many descriptive phrases in one cell. If too many descriptors, or indicators (as some prefer to label them), reside in one cell, the individual who is being rated must meet all the

Figure 2.2 A Simple IC Map

Teacher ______________________

Component 1: Selects Objectives			
(1)	*(2)*	*(3)*	*(4)*
Selects objectives, in sequence from the district list, and may add objectives to address the needs of particular students.	Identifies objectives from other published documents that cover the district list.	Refers to other sources for objectives not related to the district list.	
Component 2: Uses Materials			
(1)	*(2)*	*(3)*	*(4)*
Uses Heatherton textbook, district supplemental materials, and adds other items to increase student interest and mastery.	Stays strictly within the Heatherton textbook.	Uses other materials collected from teaching experience.	Engages randomly with no systematic set of materials.
Component 3: Engages Students in Learning			
(1)	*(2)*	*(3)*	*(4)*
Encourages students to engage in a variety of learning strategies to meet the particular objective and specific students' needs.	Leans heavily on lecture and text assignments, with students self-checking their work.	Maintains careful daily attention to the scope and sequence of the program in order to cover the materials and objectives.	

Component 4: Assesses Progress			
(1)	*(2)*	*(3)*	*(4)*
Observes students' daily work, provides weekly tests as benchmarks, and uses district assessments for final evidence of mastery.	Uses the Heatherton text's end-of-chapter tests routinely, and occasionally employs the district mastery test.	Relies on classroom observation of students' work and on teacher-constructed tests.	Employs no regular or systematic assessments.
Component 5: Identifies Next Steps			
(1)	*(2)*	*(3)*	*(4)*
Moves students who have mastered current objective to the next objective, and reteaches—using new material—those who have not mastered.	Moves all students along to the next objective in order to cover the program and/ or the textbook.		

Source: Hord & Roussin, 2013, p. 51.

items. This becomes problematic when there is an overabundance of descriptors and the individual doesn't meet all of them.

Using IC to Support the Strategies. As shared in the description of Strategy 1—Create a Shared Vision of the Change, one of the major purposes of the IC map is to provide a clear depiction of the innovation, or new practice, in operation. The first cell of each component describes the new practices in their ideal state and therefore communicates for all individuals what the behavioral expectations for the change are. With the subsequent horizontal cells, it is possible to understand how the implementers will move, across time and with help, to the ideal status.

Because the map indicates what individuals will be doing and how they will be using the innovation, it serves as an initial indicator of what implementers must learn in order to use innovations in the appropriate way. Thus, Strategy 2—Invest in Professional Learning can employ the map to target, plan, and design learning activities for the implementers. The map communicates to change leaders precisely what must be learned for successful implementation. Because the map is explicit, in Strategy 3—Plan for Implementation and Identify the Required Resources, the needs for time, material, and human resources are made clear and cannot be denied. The budget committee should have access to the map so that understanding of the implementers' needs is revealed early and can be arranged.

Strategy 4—Monitor Progress is the formative assessment of progress that is made by the implementer across time. The IC map is an invaluable tool to use for this purpose. At the time of the assessment of the implementer's progress (or regression), the change facilitator involves the implementer in a collegial conversation in order to collaboratively identify where the implementer is on the components of the map, using the map as the standard for implementation. This assessment is done thoughtfully and sensitively so that the assessment decision is shared by both. In close relation to these data generated by Strategy 4 is the use of these data for Strategy 5—Provide Ongoing Assistance. This assistance is the identification of a supportive intervention that will help the implementer move closer to the ideal description of innovation use. Since the IC map is a growth-inducing tool, it should be used by the facilitator in such a way as to accept where on the continuum the implementer currently is placed, with an appropriate suggestion that encourages the implementer and stimulates action and movement to improved practice, as defined in the ideal cell. The IC map was never intended primarily for evaluative purposes, but rather as a tool to illuminate and facilitate teachers', principals', or other implementers' growth toward the ideal.

In Strategy 6—Create a Context Conducive to Change, the IC map is used to guide appropriate approval for clear areas of strength and to identify areas for growth and improvement. It also sets the stage for the implementer's self-analysis and self-correction. The coach, or facilitator, does this while continuing trust building with the implementer. The assessing and assisting conference of Strategies 4 and 5 with the implementer also supports the implementer's confidence, competence, and professional status, while guiding her or his appropriate use of the innovation.

Change facilitators and coaches can be of tremendous benefit to learners of new programs and for developing a context conducive to change. But the coach requires deep knowledge of the new program and well-honed skills for working as a supporting and caring individual who uses data and their analyses on which to base coaching activities. Data collection tools such as Innovation Configuration maps are essential for understanding the individual user's progress in her or his efforts to implement innovations.

Applications of the IC map include the following:

- Describing and communicating what the innovation or change is, while identifying best practices (ideal variation) of the innovation; providing a common vocabulary for dialogue and conversation about the change that promotes commitment to the change; and setting expectations for the ultimate quality use of the innovations as novices of the change move to expertise
- Clarifying the *what* of the innovation during creation of the map by potential users, thus deepening the implementers' understanding of the innovation and promoting the individual's reflection and assessment of his or her practice of the change
- Providing the means by which instructional leaders can accurately discuss the progress of implementation, identify specific resources and support needed for innovation implementation and sustainability, and provide guidance for the design of professional learning
- Providing the basis for altering or differentiating the innovation or its use over time

School and district leaders and other change facilitators frequently ask about the difference between a rubric and the IC map. Please note Figure 2.3.

Kennedy, in responding to a group of educators with whom she was working, studied this question, consulted with a number of IC users on the question of differences in a rubric and an IC map, and has offered a comparison chart. This comparison is more holistic than analytical, and general versus task specific. As she notes at the bottom of Figure 2.3, there appears to be much similarity between the rubric and the map, although the structure and voice are easily

Figure 2.3 Differences Between an Innovation Configuration Map and Rubric

Major Differences		*Innovation Configuration Map*	*Rubric*
Structure and Conventions	Range	Highest level is on the left, and lower numbers are ideal	Highest scale is on the right, and higher numbers are ideal
	Number of levels	Number of levels varies for each component (e.g., 1–4; 1–5; 1–6)	Number of levels is the same (uniform) for each
Purpose and Functions	Voice	Written in active voice (always begins with an action verb)	Written in passive voice (may include more adjectives and adverbs)
	Purpose	Describes behaviors	Describes qualities
	Focus	Focused on responsibilities of roles (often many roles) to support implementation of new practice, the innovation	Focused on student work, assessments, etc.
	Uses	Primarily intended for support and assistance; growth orientation. Used to inform what a new practice is and how to enact it.	Primarily used for evaluation of a final product

Note: These are general differences. In that rubrics take many forms, some rubrics are very similar to an Innovation Configuration map.

Source: Kennedy, 2013. Used with permission.

distinguishable. The most significant difference in these two instruments is the *uses* for which the two constructs are employed. The IC map is intended for the assistance and support of the implementer's growth—it is used to inform what a new practice is and how to enact it—while the rubric is primarily used for evaluation of a product.

The jury probably is still out on the question of rubric and IC map differences, but until more specificity is gained, Figure 2.3 is helpful in understanding the two tools.

We now give attention to a second research-based construct deemed highly useful for successfully implementing the standard of implementation.

Stages of Concern

The cornerstone of the Concerns-Based Adoption Model, Stages of Concern (SoC), has been reported by George, Hall, and Stiegelbauer (2006), with modest revisions to the original construct. This construct identifies an individual's feelings, attitudes, and perceptions about an innovation. SoC represents the personal side of change, for it reveals the affective dimension of the individual's view of implementing a change. Thus, this affective dimension can be helpful or disruptive to the process of implementation.

Seven Stages of Concern. The CBAM researchers identified and confirmed seven types or categories of concerns, with each labeled and defined by an individual's expressions or comments. Individuals perceive tasks and expectations in different ways depending on their knowledge, experience, and worldview, thus the different categories of concern. They may feel overwhelmed and confused, or threatened by the expectations of the changes to be implemented. Their concerns are typically stimulated by their perceptions, rather than by the reality of the situation.

Facilitators responsible for supporting individuals in their implementation of an innovative program, process, or practice will find it of great value to identify implementers' concerns and act to reduce or ameliorate them. The seven Stages of Concern and an individual's typical expression that identifies each stage can be viewed in Figure 2.4. Notice that the seven stages are grouped in four categories: unrelated, self, task, and impact.

Measuring Stages of Concern. But how does a facilitator or supporter of implementation gain access to an individual's SoC? There are three methods for doing this:

1. A *short interview* that appears very casual and is conducted in the implementer's office, classroom, or even during a short walk across the parking lot is conducted by the facilitator with the implementer. CBAM researchers label this short interaction a "one-legged conference," for it takes not much

Figure 2.4 The Stages of Concern About an Innovation

Stage			*Description*	*Typical Statements*
Impact	6	Refocusing	The individual focuses on exploring ways to reap more universal benefits from the innovation, including the possibility of making major changes to it or replacing it with a more powerful alternative.	I have some ideas about something that would work even better.
	5	Collaboration	The individual focuses on coordinating and cooperating with others regarding the use of the innovation.	I'd like to work with others who are also using this innovation.
	4	Consequence	The individual focuses on the innovation's impact on the students in his or her immediate sphere of influence. Considerations include the relevance of the innovation to students; the evaluation of student outcomes, including performance and competencies; and the changes needed to improve student outcomes.	I'm wondering how this innovation is affecting my students.
Task	3	Management	The individual focuses on the processes and tasks of using the innovation and the best use of information and resources. Issues related to efficiency, organizing, managing, and scheduling dominate.	I seem to be spending all of my time getting material ready.

Stage			Description	Typical Statements
Self	2	Personal	The individual is uncertain about the demands of the innovation, his or her adequacy to meet those demands, and/or his or her role with the innovation. The individual is analyzing his or her relationship to the reward structure of the organization, determining his or her part in decision making, and considering potential conflicts with existing structures or personal commitment. Concerns also might involve the financial or status implications of the program for the individual and his or her colleagues.	I'm concerned that using this innovation will mean I have to change my established routines.
	1	Informational	The individual indicates a general awareness of the innovation and interest in learning more details about it. The individual does not seem to be worried about himself or herself in relation to the innovation. Any interest is in impersonal, substantive aspects of the innovation, such as its general characteristics, effects, and requirements for use.	I would like to learn more about this innovation.
	0	Unconcerned	The individual indicates little concern about or involvement with the innovation.	I have other things to do that are more important to me.

Source: From *Measuring Implementation in Schools: The Stages of Concern Questionnaire* (p. 8), by A. A. George, G. E. Hall, and S. M. Stiegelbauer, 2006, Austin, TX: SEDL. Copyright © 2006 by SEDL. Reprinted by Corwin and Learning Forward with permission from SEDL.

more time than one can stand on one leg. Through practice one can become quite adept at simple questions and conversation that elicit data to be analyzed and identify the implementer's concern(s). Such opener questions include the following:

How is it going with you and the new language arts program?

How are you thinking about, or feeling about, the mathematics curriculum that the district just adopted?

2. An *open-ended statement* approach is a second means for gaining concerns data. Implementers are asked to write several complete sentences that describe their concerns, which are then content analyzed. Those responding to this approach are asked questions such as these on a blank sheet of paper:

   When you think about the student engagement practices (or whatever the innovation is), what concerns do you have?

   Please be candid and frank, and answer in complete sentences.

3. The third means for collecting SoC data is through the *35-item questionnaire* that is employed for research and evaluation purposes; therefore it will not be given attention here. For further information, see Hall and Hord (2015).

Using SoC to Support the Strategies. How might concerns data derived from one of the data gathering approaches described above be used to support the strategies?

SoC data can be most fruitfully used for Strategy 2—Invest in Professional Learning in planning and designing learning for implementers. Large-group learning sessions for a schoolwide group, or another group of initial implementers, will likely target the implementers' informational (SoC 1) and personal (SoC 2) concerns. These individuals are just becoming aware of and learning about the new program or practices they will be expected to use. Therefore, enabling them to learn about the "new" will likely be needed for all. But as implementers move into getting acquainted with and using the innovative practices, their learning needs will become divergent. In addition to using the IC map to understand what they are doing with the innovation, the SoC will reveal implementers' concerns as they become active with the innovation. Many will move beyond SoC 1 and 2, but always there are some who become entrenched in personal concerns and will need facilitative support to move beyond this.

It is safe to say that almost all new users will have management concerns (SoC 3), and these concerns about time and how to organize the new program will remain unless implementers are provided with clear and "just in time" learning that helps them resolve these concerns and move toward lower-intensity SoC 3 concerns or to consequence concerns (SoC 4). Data that reveal collaboration concerns (SoC 5) serve as a useful indicator of implementers' interests in working together to increase benefits for their students and, thus, needs for learning about how to collaborate.

For Strategy 4—Monitor Progress, SoC data are rich indicators of how implementers are reacting to and feeling about their progress with the new practices. Change facilitators, who recognize these various concerns and their impact on implementers, use these data to support the implementer in appropriate ways (Strategy 5—Provide Ongoing Assistance). This assistance is expected to address and respond to a particular concern. Implementers recognize the interest and actions that facilitators take to support and assist them, and in this way, a context conducive to change (Strategy 6) is expanded.

Levels of Use

While Stages of Concern was the initial concept studied by the R&D Center staff, a second was created when further research revealed a new dimension for describing implementers as they engaged in the process of change efforts in K–12 schools and colleges. This construct, Levels of Use, is the third tool to be used for implementing professional learning and successful change.

Eight Levels of Use. Learning about *what* the change is is a necessary precondition to using it in classrooms or its intended setting. *How* implementers are using the innovation (or perhaps, not using it) is the focus of Levels of Use (Hall, Dirksen, & George, 2006). Many school and district leaders assume that delivering the required new materials and supplying an initial 2-day learning session will enable all implementers to put new programs and practices into satisfactory use. This belief was challenged by the researchers as they launched studies to identify descriptions, and the implications, of a wide variety of "using" the innovation and the variables that determined these differences.

Beware of confusing the two concepts, Stages of Concern and Levels of Use, and the labels that attend each—they have a deceptively similar sound. SoC reflects the affective side of change: the individual's reactions, perceptions, feelings, and attitudes. LoU addresses the behaviors and describes how individuals are acting with a particular change. These behaviors can be observed as individuals endeavor to learn about and master new practices. As potential implementers adopt, initiate, and become active in implementation, their behaviors are observed and described, resulting in the identification and explanation of eight Levels of Use. As with SoC, identifying and understanding an individual's LoU makes it possible to provide helpful assistance and facilitation for his or her improved use of the new practice.

Figure 2.5 describes the eight levels and a brief example of a typical statement about each. Notice the eight levels are arranged in two groups: nonusers and users.

Measuring LoU. How does a coach, principal, or lead teacher—any of whom are facilitating implementation—determine at which LoU an implementer is operating? Unlike SoC, which has three strong procedures (interviewing, open-ended statements, and a survey) by which to identify implementers' Stages of Concern, Levels of Use has one method: interviewing. There are two protocols for the interviews. One is for identifying an individual's overall LoU through an *informal conversation* (reminiscent of the one-legged conference of SoC). The other is a *more demanding interview* used for research and evaluation purposes, requiring intensive training of the interviewer; this results in a complex array of factors and variables that are rated by the interviewer subsequent to the interview. This latter procedure will not be discussed here, for this is a chapter about facilitating implementation and not about evaluating it, although the concepts and constructs and their measures could be employed for evaluation.

The interview process used for supporting and tracking the implementer's use is the informal one-legged conversation, using the sequenced questions shown in the branching technique in Figure 2.6.

Depending on the response to the first question, the individual is cited "Yes" as a user or "No" as not a user. This response dictates the branch to be followed for the remainder of the conversation. Each question serves the interviewer in refining the possibilities for the

Figure 2.5 Levels of Use of an Innovation

	Level		Description	Typical Statement
Users	VI	Renewal	User reevaluates the quality of use of the innovation, seeks major modifications or alternatives to the present innovation to achieve increased impact on clients, examines new developments in the field, and explores new goals for self and the system.	As department chair, I've used interim assessments and found that they really help with student understanding. They also help me know how each student is progressing. Now I'm looking into a computerized system that will administer the tests, keep each student's record, and compile a class profile.
	V	Integration	User is combining own efforts to use the innovation with the related activities of colleagues to achieve a collective effect on clients in their common sphere of influence.	In the fall, Joan and I decided to use the same interim assessments with our freshman English classes. We are now able to compare how well students are learning the benchmarks. My students did not do as well as Joan's in two areas. So this term, I'm using Joan's lesson plans to see if my students will do better.
	IVB	Refinement	User varies the use of the innovation to increase the impact on clients in the immediate sphere of influence. Variations are based on knowledge of both short- and long-term consequences for clients.	I've compiled the data from the assessments that I used last term. I see that some of my students consistently perform lower, but I believe that they really have learned the material. As I check into it, I see a pattern: Those students who do not read as well are not performing as well on my interim assessments. I'm now going to develop and try some assessments that do not rely on reading.

(Continued)

Figure 2.5 (Continued)

	Level		*Description*	*Typical Statement*
Users	IVA	Routine	Use of the innovation is stabilized. Few if any changes are being made in ongoing use. Little preparation or thought is being given to improving innovation use or its consequences.	I'm using interim assessments the same way this year that I did last year. I have a bank of them and can pull out the most appropriate ones to use as I go along. I see them as important to knowing what my students understand. I find that my assessments correlate well with how my students do on the state tests.
	III	Mechanical Use	User focuses most effort on the short-term, day-to-day use of the innovation with little time for reflection. Changes in use are made more to meet user needs than client needs. The user is primarily engaged in a stepwise attempt to master the tasks required to use the innovation, often resulting in disjointed and superficial use.	I'm spending at least 2 hours every weekend developing interim assessments to use in the coming week. Some of my assessments have worked, but several have been confusing to my students. I've had to rework those plus build the new ones for the subsequent weeks. I also developed some that I never had time to use.

	Level		Description	Typical Statement
Nonusers	II	Preparation	User is preparing for first use of the innovation.	Well, our principal has decided that all of us teachers will do interim assessments. I've bought two books about interim assessments and found several useful sites on the web. These sites have provided several assessments that I think I can use and are helping me to prepare to use the assessments next term.
	I	Orientation	User has acquired or is acquiring information about the innovation and/or has explored or is exploring its value orientation and its demands on the user and the user system.	I attended a workshop on the importance of interim assessments. I'm thinking about them, but haven't decided to include them in my teaching. I have talked with my department chair and one of my teaching colleagues about them.
	0	Nonuse	User has little or no knowledge of the innovation, has no involvement with the innovation, and is doing nothing toward becoming involved.	I don't know anything about the new interim assessments. I haven't talked with anyone about them and don't have any plans to do so. I remember someone mentioning them in the faculty meeting, but I didn't pay any attention to what was said.

Note: In a modest effort to distinguish SoC from LoU, Arabic numerals are used for the labels of Stages of Concern while Roman numerals are employed for the Levels of Use.

Source: © Sonia Caus Gleason. Used with permission.

Figure 2.6 The Branching Technique

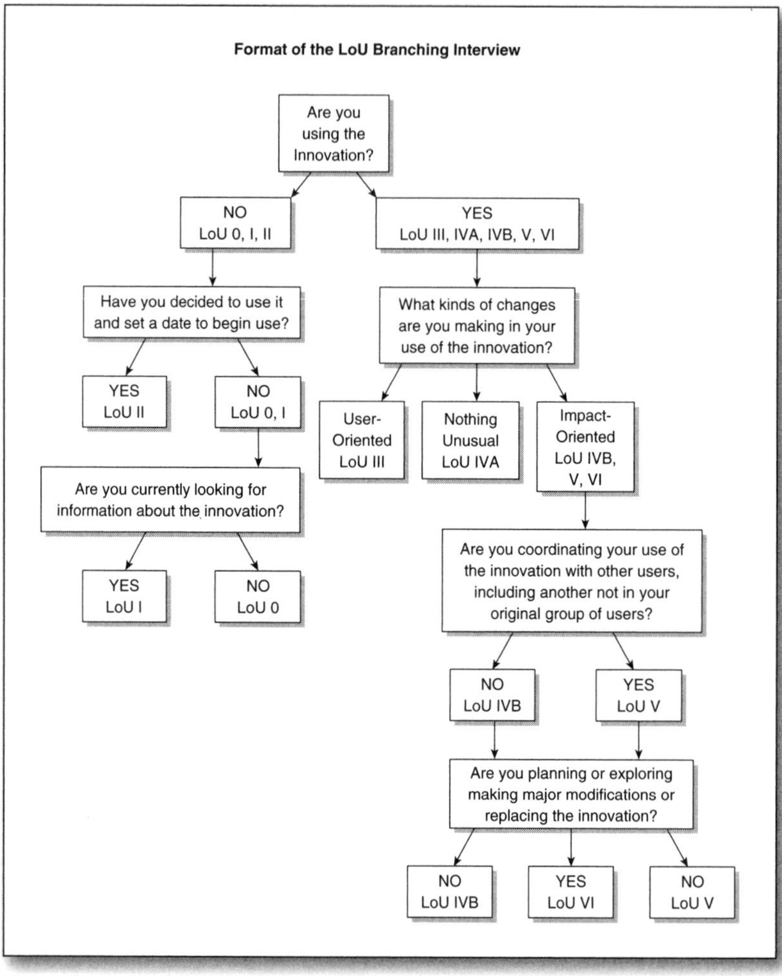

Source: From *Measuring Implementation in Schools: Levels of Use* (p. 18), by G. E. Hall, D. J. Dirksen, and A. A. George, 2006, Austin, TX: SEDL. Copyright © 2006 by SEDL. Reprinted by Corwin and Learning Forward with permission from SEDL.

individual's specific LoU. Needless to say, the use of this interview protocol requires deep learning and practice; it is not intended to be used by novice interviewers.

Using LoU to Support the Strategies. How can Levels of Use data be employed to increase the power of the strategies?

When change leaders have access to implementers' LoU, the Strategy 2—Invest in Professional Learning can be planned and designed to address where the implementers are in their implementation journey. That is, if a participant is at preparation (LoU II), then learning sessions can be provided to support the implementer in making the preparations necessary for the innovation. If mechanical (LoU III) is indicated, then learning for this implementer focuses on helping him or her organize materials, carefully allot time, and arrange tasks so that using the innovation proceeds smoothly.

For Strategy 4—Monitor Progress, LoU data can be used to help the coach or facilitator analyze the implementer's needs and make decisions for appropriate support or help (Strategy 5—Provide Ongoing Assistance). If the implementer's data show integration (LoU V), the facilitator assists in arranging structures so that the implementer is able to work with other implementers to use the innovation in ways that further benefit their students (Strategy 5—Providing Ongoing Assistance). If the data indicate routine (LoU IVA), the facilitator may determine to take some action to stimulate the implementer to a higher Level of Use (Strategy 4—Monitoring Progress and "pushing" to greater progress). The facilitator does this while continuing trust building with the implementer.

The suggestions and applications of the six strategies and the three tools have been modestly drawn. But they reveal the array of implementation issues and possibilities that principals, central office personnel, lead teachers, coaches, and others may encounter in the real-life activities of successful change efforts. The focus has been on how the strategies and tools may be fruitfully used to support and assist successful implementation. For further information about the *what* and the *how* of these strategies and tools, see Hord and Roussin (2013).

In Conclusion

This chapter's goal has been to articulate the imperative of implementing professional *learning* as the basis for *change* in a school, district, or other organization, which leads to *improvement* of practice. To reflect this truth, a banner or bumper sticker would read

Learning >> Change >> Improvement

Standards for creating high-quality learning have been identified by Learning Forward in its newly revised standards (2011), and all of these standards are necessary for effective and successful professional learning.

A basic premise found throughout all the change process constructs and their measures identified and described in this chapter, as well as the strategies specified and described for change, is that learning is an absolute for change to occur. The learning by educators through effective, standards-based professional learning influences and changes their classroom practices, which, in turn, impacts students.

Most assuredly, a major theme and essential understanding found across Michael Fullan's opening chapter as well as this chapter is the grounding that change is synonymous with learning. It is that simple, but also that complex.

In this sixth Standard for Professional Learning, Implementation, Learning Forward encourages and supports all educators with the understanding that professional learning must be *implemented* in its intended setting if it is to maximize opportunities for every student to achieve. To give added meaning to this standard, Learning Forward articulated three directives:

- Apply change research, which has been done lavishly in this chapter.
- Provide constructive feedback, which has been suggested throughout, but most emphatically in Strategy 4—Monitor Progress.
- Sustain implementation; this message has been repeated and repeated, in appeals for time, attention, and other resources to sustain the implementation challenge so that new practices may be realized in classrooms and students may learn successfully.

Our schools and our students deserve no less.

References

Collins, J. (2001). *Good to great: Why some companies make the leap and others don't.* New York, NY: HarperCollins.

Cuban, L. (2013). *Inside the black box of classroom practice.* Cambridge, MA: Harvard University Press.

George, A. A., Hall, G. E., & Stiegelbauer, S. M. (2006). *Measuring implementation in schools: The Stages of Concern Questionnaire.* Austin, TX: Southwest Educational Development Laboratory.

Hall, G. E., Dirksen, D. J. & George, A. A. (2006). *Measuring implementation in schools: Levels of use.* Austin, TX: Southwest Educational Development Laboratory.

Hall, G. E., & Hord, S. M. (2015). *Implementing change: Patterns, principles, and potholes* (4th ed.). Upper Saddle River, NJ: Pearson.

Hord, S. M., & Roussin, J. L. (2013). *Implementing change through learning: Concerns-based concepts, tools, and strategies for guiding change.* Thousand Oaks, CA: Corwin.

Hord, S. M., Stiegelbauer, S. M., Hall, G. E., & George, A. A. (2006). *Measuring implementation in schools: Innovation configurations.* Austin, TX: Southwest Educational Development Laboratory.

Joyce, B., & Showers, B. (2002). *Student achievement through staff development* (3rd ed.). Alexandria, VA: Association for Supervision and Curriculum Development.

Kennedy, J. (2013). *Differences between an innovation configuration map and rubric.* Oxford, OH: Learning Forward.

Learning Forward. (2011). *Standards for professional learning.* Oxford, OH: Author.

Tschannen-Moran, M. (2004). *Trust matters: Leadership for successful schools.* San Francisco, CA: Jossey-Bass.

Chapter Three

The Case Study

Valerie von Frank

USING THIS CASE STUDY

Most readers of this case study will find a district that is different from theirs. The temptation is to say this district is too rich or more disadvantaged, larger or smaller, more urban, more rural, more or less diverse. Doing so misses the value of a case study.

The questions at the heart of the matter are about how well this system stands up when we consider the major strands of this specific standard for professional learning. In reading the case study, it's fair to ask how the system meets the individual standard, as well as in what ways it may not. It's helpful to consider how well the district meets the other standards for professional learning, which top-performing systems generally do because of the interconnected nature of the standards. Most effective systems working to achieve one standard strive toward quality professional learning that meets multiple standards. But in the real world, as they reach, they also may fall short in one area or another.

The decision for this series to use real, journalistic-style rather than fictionalized case studies was deliberate. The intent is for readers to hear educators' voices from actual practice, to see examples of what is possible and what it looks like to work to the level of a specific standard for professional learning—including some aspects that may not fully exemplify the standard. The districts were chosen based on research, interviews, and solid evidence that student outcomes are improving, because student achievement is the ultimate goal of professional learning. Professional learning does not take place for its own sake, but to enable teachers to teach effectively so that every student achieves.

Often these days it seems we are tempted to focus on our differences rather than seeking the good we can find in the model before us. Reading a case study should invite that certain amount of critique, but also of recognition if not admiration. Rather than losing the point by focusing on differences and perceived shortcomings, we invite you to consider the standard at hand. Review its main components. Ask how this district exemplifies those elements. Listen carefully to what those at each level of the system said about learning from their vantage point.

Ask probing questions, either as a reader or with colleagues, and use the case as it is meant—for thoughtful discussion of a district's strengths, areas for improvement, and more than as a comparison with your own or an ideal, as a launching point for discussing how the standard for professional learning strengthens educators' core work and makes possible greater student achievement. When you have delved deeply into the standard itself, the next step is to look within your own district to determine how the standard can be used to improve your system.

At the end of the case study, you will find a set of discussion questions to prime your reflection, analysis, and discussion. We encourage you to meet and discuss this district's implementation of professional learning with a few colleagues and share your insights with other school and district staff.

> *Though there have been changes in the system's priorities and approach, these have been the result of evolution, not revolution. Long Beach's culture of consultation, the collective ownership of its schools, data-driven decision making, and the focus on what students learn rather than what teachers teach are all deeply embedded in the system.*
>
> —Mourshed, Chijioke, & Barber (2010, p. 89)

Hamilton Middle School language arts department chair Karrie Lourenco was thrilled when she had opportunities to observe teachers in her department within the school day. She was also surprised by what she found.

At the beginning of the year, the department's teachers had set their individual learning goals, aligning the goals with school and district objectives based on student data. The language arts teachers agreed that all would work on students' skills in citing texts. They also agreed to work with students on listening skills and working collaboratively. The teachers discussed what they would see when they were trying new strategies and how to recognize effective practices.

So when Lourenco visited a classroom and saw, among other things, students sitting in neat rows facing the teacher in front of the room, she saw a knowing-doing gap.

"We assume that when we're sitting and talking we're all on the same page," Lourenco said. "It was interesting for me to find out that we weren't. Teachers said they were implementing the strategies, so it was a lack of understanding of what the expectations were."

These walk-throughs are one of the strategies Long Beach (California) Unified School District (LBUSD) leaders use to support teacher learning and follow up on the implementation of new initiatives, and one way the internal culture of continuous learning is sustained.

Walk-Throughs

Schools throughout this large urban system regularly use walk-throughs for learning—both to gauge what support teachers need and for observers to learn about others' practices. Along with visits like Lourenco's, school teams and administrators regularly observe in less structured visits. Formally, the district groups multiple schools, and teams from these schools visit one another.

> Long Beach is located near Los Angeles and has the nation's busiest port. Long Beach Unified School District has 84 campuses in the cities of Long Beach, Lakewood, Signal Hill, and Avalon on Catalina Island, including 12 high schools, 17 middle schools, and 56 elementary and K–8 schools. The third largest school district in California, it serves a diverse population. Students come from homes where any of 50 different languages are spoken. Total enrollment is 82,256 students, with 70% eligible for free or reduced-price meals. Its student population is 15.3% African American, 12.6% Asian/Pacific Islander, 54.4% Hispanic, 14.7% White, and 2.9% other.

Hamilton principal Kathleen Cruz and her assistant principal spend time daily observing teachers' classrooms. Cruz said the assistant principal spends more than half his day visiting classrooms, particularly those in which management is an issue. She regularly stops into three to four different rooms each day to observe for up to a half hour at a time.

"It gives me a really good handle in terms of what I've done at the faculty meeting and if that learning is being implemented correctly," Cruz said. "So it gives me that opportunity to step back and see if I need to reteach or do something a little different if I'm seeing sitewide that the implementation isn't working."

Cruz then leaves immediate feedback in the teachers' mailboxes on what practices she observed that are in line with schoolwide goals. "And I always also try to either ask a question or push for growth in a certain area," she said.

In addition, four times a year, central office support personnel accompany Cruz in what she terms "informal walk-throughs" that might look at how teachers in one grade level or content area are implementing new practices. For example, Cruz said a district walk-through revealed a gap between her expectation and classroom practice: "One of the things that we are working on this year is learning targets, which is a shift for people. In one of the district walk-throughs we did, we found learning targets weren't focused on the level of cognition expected of an assignment.

"After the district team left, my assistant principal and I went into every classroom and recorded the learning targets, because we wanted to have a better understanding of what we were seeing. Then, I published in a bulletin that goes out weekly to teachers just some of the learning targets that we had seen that were focused, that were right on. We gave teachers some examples—without names attached. I know that learning targets now are going to be covered in departmental meetings."

If the concern continues, Cruz said, she meets individually with teachers to discuss what a learning target is and missing pieces, and to brainstorm appropriate learning targets.

In the districtwide process, three to four principals, along with district curriculum leaders and at least one director or assistant superintendent, visit schools in the cohort at least three times a year, in fall, winter, and spring. Teams spend up to 10 minutes at a time in as many classrooms as possible in a visit that lasts approximately three hours. The process begins with a brief orientation at the hosting school.

"The school identifies what they want the team to look at, what facet of implementation they're working on," said Pamela Seki, director of curriculum, instruction, and professional development. The team members don't identify individual classrooms but give feedback on trends using a districtwide protocol. In prior years, some principals had included teachers on these visitation teams. In 2013–2014, the district revised the process to formally include teachers.

Lourenco stresses that team members leave clipboards and protocols outside when they enter the classroom. They observe and talk to students, then make notes on the district form once they have left the classroom, without identifying a class or teacher in order to reduce the appearance of an evaluation and lessen the teacher's stress of being observed. That takes away a bit of the evaluative feel of the visits, she said.

Jill Baker, assistant superintendent, elementary and K–8 schools, and chief academic officer, said the walk-throughs are "not intended to be a review of the school or telling people what they're not doing, but simply to say, 'On this given day, here are examples of what we saw that we think match what we expect to see, here are the celebrations that we saw, and here are some things to think about.'"

Lourenco, a 12-year veteran, said teachers have simply come to expect the possibility that a team will drop in. The practice, she said, keeps her always on her A-game, constantly striving to be at her best.

Learning Up, Down, and Across

LBUSD Superintendent Christopher Steinhauser said that walk-throughs are a prime source of information to make course correction districtwide as changes are implemented: "You have to continually look at the feedback loop that you're getting from your evaluation of your professional learning, the walk-throughs that you're doing, so that if there are missteps along the way, you can correct those right away and fine-tune those."

Feedback from walk-throughs is sent to district committees so that curriculum leaders and school supervisors can refine districtwide professional development. For example, the district recognized it wasn't able to efficiently support professional learning in writing because schools were implementing different approaches. Administrators decided a districtwide approach was in order in this instance. They offered schools an option to join in a cohort, giving participating schools a dedicated, part-time coach on site and release time for teachers to look at student work and take part in the professional development. Four cohorts later, every teacher in K–5 is using the program and engaging in continual improvement around writing.

Next, administrators looked at the middle schools and required participation from each school designated as needing improvement.

The success and improved student achievement at those schools led other middle schools into the fold.

Now teachers at the high school have found that incoming students are using the thinking maps strategy they learned in the lower grades in the writing program. So the district has begun to train high school teachers to use thinking maps as a writing approach.

The district considers every opportunity to continually tweak the way professional learning occurs. When state funding cuts cost LBUSD approximately $330 million over just a handful of years, leaders found ways to make changes to the transportation schedule to save money. They simultaneously seized on the opportunity to coordinate elementary school schedules so that all the elementary teachers have 40 minutes of planning time on the same day every week.

Budget cuts have also meant greater emphasis on school-based learning, less coaching, and a tightly planned model for how knowledge passes to school-level staff. Rather than systemwide professional development, the district has shifted to a cadre of lead teachers and principals who are instructional leaders. As a districtwide committee planned how to roll out learning around the Common Core State Standards, for example, members studied research then mapped out the content and staff roles and responsibilities in order to create greater coherence and clarity around professional learning. The sequence of learning for teachers was set alongside the sequence for principals.

To shift to more site-based learning, each elementary school designated a language arts and a math lead teacher at lower and upper elementary who learn from a full day of professional development with district curriculum leaders about expectations, what changes should be seen in classroom teacher behavior, and timelines. The lead teachers receive what the district calls a "trainer's tool kit" with PowerPoint slides, handouts, a script, and supporting materials. Those teachers share the information with colleagues at their schools, gather teacher feedback and student work, and then come back together to share before repeating the cycle.

These teachers spend a full day each trimester, while secondary department heads are in a daylong summer institute and meet together for 2 hours six times a year. Principals take part in separate, aligned learning and receive their own training modules to use at their sites. The district then uses curriculum pacing guides that let teachers know which objectives they should be teaching at what times.

Professional learning is tied to that timing.

"It doesn't help in implementation to have a high school principal go out looking for something in January [walk-throughs] that the teachers have not learned about," Baker said.

Teachers are responsible for analyzing the data from quarterly common assessments of student learning to consider ways to improve their practices. Lourenco said she meets weekly with her colleagues in professional learning around curriculum: "Our district is amazing at deconstructing the maze and giving it to us in chunks. Our department talks about what we tried in the classroom, discusses what's working, what's not working, and what we need to tweak. Then we go back to the classroom and tweak as needed, and come back together again."

For example, Lourenco said a recent department meeting was about differences between formative and interim assessments as well as gauging the complexity of the text students are using in order to empower teachers to pick a quality text that matches Common Core standards.

Lourenco also meets with her colleagues in grade-level team meetings for "business" and to discuss individual students and student work.

In faculty meetings, the principal reinforces district objectives with the training modules she was given in district professional development sessions. At Hamilton, faculty meetings alternate between the principal and lead teachers leading the professional learning. When lead teachers focus on professional learning in these meetings, faculty break into subject matter groups to home in on Common Core expectations in English, math, or literacy.

"So we have three separate groups in the meeting," Cruz said, "and then the next meeting will be a whole-faculty meeting, and then after that the Common Core lead teacher. I'm able to present general information, and then with the lead teacher, it's much more specific."

"There are roles in professional development for multiple people," Baker said. "We want to create a lot of learning opportunities but also not feel like teachers are going through professional development or sessions with their principals, in particular, that are duplicates of what they are learning in other arenas. And so we've defined, here's the piece that we want to help principals feel comfortable in teaching to their staff, here's the piece that lead teachers from every school are going to engage with the district and then take back to their school site to lead, here's a piece that we can actually afford to have direct contact with every teacher, and then they are taking that knowledge directly to their classroom. So there's a mapping of responsibilities and content knowledge, and a lot of it happens simultaneously. We have pushed toward collaboration at the site level, where teams of people, to some degree in professional learning communities, are all working together to bring about learning and bring coherence at the site level."

A CYCLE OF CONTINUOUS IMPROVEMENT

A culture of continuous improvement has led to higher student achievement recognized over many years by multiple organizations:

- The district was one of five named as the world's highest-performing school systems in a 2012 report by Battelle for Kids, which cited districts that showed "more than five consistent rises in student performance across multiple data points" (p. 4). According to the report, "the culture of high expectations is followed through at all levels" (p. 19).
- In 2012, fifteen district schools were named to the California Business for Education Excellence Honor Roll for academic excellence and reducing achievement gaps among student populations.
- A report from McKinsey & Company (Mourshed et al., 2010) cites the district as a world leader, placing it among the top 20 systems globally for continuous improvement.
- LBUSD was awarded the Broad Prize in 2003, in addition to being a four-time finalist–in 2002, 2007, 2008, and 2009. As the 2009 Broad Prize fact sheet states, "This is the essence of the Long Beach Way–methodical improvement, with ongoing modifications to professional development and student support as called for by student data" (Broad Prize for Urban Education, 2009, p. 6).

"The culture really is: How do we learn from ourselves?" said Baker. "We are students of the organization. We always have to see things as opportunities to learn."

New Initiatives Come From All

Baker said district-level committees around new initiatives such as the Common Core are "a collaborative and critical juncture for having a common vision and common goals about what we want to have happen in our schools." Those common goals are represented in the district's strategic plan, based on data. Other initiatives have bubbled up from a teacher's successful practice in support of district objectives.

Steinhauser is particularly proud of the district's work to improve students' math skills. One of the district's four goals in its 2011–2016 strategic plan states, "All students will attain proficiency in the core content areas." As two objectives to meet that goal, the district set out to increase the percentage of eighth graders enrolled in algebra by 3% each year over the five years of the plan and the percentage who achieved proficiency by a total of 5% over the plan's duration (Long Beach Unified School District, 2011).

The district was able to achieve its 2016 goal three years early, increasing the portion of students enrolled in algebra from 35% to 62% by 2013 and the percentage of proficient students from 64% to 73% in the same period, while the state's proficiency rate is around the 50% mark.

"And what's most important to me," Steinhauser said, "is that the ethnic breakdown of the kids in eighth-grade algebra matched 100% to the ethnic breakdown of the district, not only by ethnicity but by poverty. Those are huge gap-closer issues that affect student learning, and it all goes back to professional development. It's tied to resource development, coaches for math teachers, and professional development offerings."

The goal affects not only eighth graders but the system as a whole, because hundreds more students now are progressing into geometry and Algebra II. Each high school, along with middle schools that data show need support, is assigned a coach.

"It goes back to the whole gestalt of professional learning," Steinhauser said. "What I love about our system is that we have these goals, we use the data to refine the goals, and we continue to improve upon those goals. It's all about how we become better."

District leaders say much of students' improvement in math—gains of 20% to 75% in second through fifth grades from 2004 to 2009, started with one teacher who modeled his instruction on his aunt's teaching in Singapore. When colleagues at his school noticed, they emulated the approach. When the school's data improved, the district offered struggling schools an opportunity to learn about the instructional methods. The growth those schools had in students' end-of-year assessments was noted by other schools, even those with different populations.

"It caught everyone's attention," Seki said. "It was dramatic."

The instructional strategies now have spread to elementary schools systemwide.

"We tend to go slow to go fast, go small to go big," Seki said. "Almost always it is the success that brings people in."

Steinhauser said understanding the change process is imperative: "We always talk about that. We talk about resilience and how that's a critical piece of the change process, how some people will handle change, be very supportive, and move very quickly. Others will be totally resistant, and then you have the whole gamut in the middle.

"We really talk about learning theory," he continued, "as well as what's best for kids, and we bring those worlds together. We don't just march ahead and pray that everyone's with us. When people see that it's a safe zone to fail as well as succeed, then that's where true learning comes about."

The Seeds of Learning

Lourenco said some of her best learning occurred this year when she and fellow sixth-grade teachers gathered with student papers based on a district writing prompt to score the work together and develop anchor papers in a half-day of release time. They scored the papers individually and then calibrated the scoring; when scores varied more than half a point, teachers discussed the differences to understand the standards and what to look for in the student work.

"They actually paid us to go sit in a room together and score our papers together, which is amazing," Lourenco said. Seventh- and eighth-grade papers are scored at a district level to give teachers an opportunity to discuss the curriculum.

Steinhauser touted this example as "the most powerful learning and, I would say, accountability system."

"I'm not there telling them they have to do A, B, and C," he said. "They're telling themselves, based on the data, what's working well and what's not working well. That's how you build support systems from the classroom teachers to departments to the schools to the system."

Steinhauser said "no one-hit wonder" is responsible for school and district improvement. "It's all about a systems approach; it's all about supporting that from the district central office to the principals to the teachers to the students to the parents. We have worked hard to align all these processes."

Seki said the system's educators teach one another how to improve based on what they see occurring in their own classrooms and schools: "The biggest driver for us is we have a culture of continuous improvement. That culture has seeded the ground."

THE VIEW FROM THREE ROLES

CHRISTOPHER STEINHAUSER, superintendent

Teachers will tell us, "We need X." "We need Y." And it's my job to make sure all these folks running these programs have the support they need from me and from the Board of Education.

I think that what makes our culture different is that we know that we're all in this together. We're a very flat system. We all like to be in the trenches. We all know it's about how to support students, and we know that by going through the angle of support, we are going to go much faster than if we go through the angle of what a lot of places do—what I call the big stick accountability piece. Because that's not how you improve lives. That's not only for principals and teachers. That's for kids, too.

This doesn't mean that if someone, with all the support we've given them, doesn't do his or her job, that they're not held accountable. They are, and folks know that. They also know that we are going to be side by side with them all the way through, and we're going to deploy resources based on need. The site accountability expectations are extremely high here, but there's a lot of support. So some of our lowest-performing schools are going to get much more support than other schools, but we're all marching down the same road. And when things improve, those resources are realigned on a regular basis. So I think that's where people value what we do in Long Beach.

KARRIE LOURENCO, Hamilton Middle School language arts teacher

As teachers, we do a lot of talking things out and seeking others out to say, "OK, what are you doing to make this work?" We collaborate, making sure that we're listening to each other, and we're all doing the same thing. Not verbatim, but we're all expected to reach the same goals.

(Continued)

(Continued)

If all of my kids are not doing something, I have to figure out where the learning isn't taking place. I haven't seen anyone at my site discard that key question of "Why aren't my kids doing OK? What's missing here?"

We know that we're being held accountable. I think there is a certain level of expectation that Long Beach promotes so that teachers say, "We have to keep up with what's going on in our profession, because we have so many people who look at us." It might only be once a quarter, or once every quarter and a half, but we constantly have people coming to our rooms, and there is a certain level of thinking, "You know, people are coming through; I have to be on my A-game." It's so common that it doesn't faze us, but we notice it.

So I think it does come down to your work ethic. If your students are doing well as a group, you realize it has to be you as the teacher.

KATHLEEN CRUZ, Alexander Hamilton Middle School principal

The school leaders are necessary pieces in terms of continuing to move forward and in gauging where assistance is needed. Between the assistant principal and myself, we are the assurance that changes are being implemented, whether it's through walk-throughs or attending the department meetings. That gives us an idea whether strategies are being implemented and also where teachers are experiencing difficulty.

The leadership team meets weekly. Part of the meeting is feedback: What did we hear this week? Is there assistance needed? Where do people feel they are? We'll talk about grade levels, any concerns and frustrations, and what we need to do to be able to assist. We always go over anything we're seeing on campus trendwise, whether it's with behavior from kids or whether it's with faculty, that we may have concerns about. For example, we just had a district administrator who wanted to walk around with our assistant principal, so we'll discuss what they saw, what they didn't see, and where we need to move. We'll talk about our grade-level meetings for next week and what's on the agenda, and we'll make sure that we have some common pieces that every grade level will address.

Note: Quoted material from Jill Baker, Kathleen Cruz, Karrie Lourenco, Pamela Seki, and Christopher Steinhauser is used with permission.

Case Study Discussion Questions

1. How does Long Beach communicate expectations about professional learning to staff?
2. Who supports implementation of new initiatives in Long Beach?
3. How do staff get feedback about implementation?
4. Which of the other Standards for Professional Learning can we find evidence of in this case study? How do the other standards relate to and support implementation?
5. How do Long Beach's communication of, support for, and feedback about implementation compare with our district? What do we do well? In what areas can we improve?
6. What intrigues us about Long Beach's approach to professional learning?
7. What additional information do we need for evidence of how this system meets the standard?
8. What actions must we take to meet the standard for implementation?

References

Battelle for Kids. (2012). *Global education study: Six drivers of student success: A look inside five of the world's highest-performing school systems.* Retrieved from http://www.lbschools.net/District/pdf/BFK_GES_Monograph_2012.pdf

Broad Prize for Urban Education. (2009). *Long Beach Unified School District, Calif.: District profile.* Retrieved from http://www.broadprize.org/asset/1334-tbp2009factsheetlong%20beach.pdf

Long Beach Unified School District. (2011). *Long Beach Unified School District strategic plan 2011–2016.* Retrieved from http://www.lbusd.k12.ca.us/Main_Offices/Superintendent/Strategic_Planning

Mourshed, M., Chijioke, C., & Barber, M. (2010). *How the world's most improved school systems keep getting better.* London, England: McKinsey.

Figure 3.1 Protocol Form for Walk-Throughs

long beach unified school district

Toward Full Implementation – ES/MS/K–8 School Walk-through Protocol

Fall 2013

Purpose: To reinforce and learn from classroom efforts related to the full implementation of the Common Core State Standards in the areas of English Language Arts, Mathematics and/or Transitions in Pedagogy.
Logistics: This walk-through process will be conducted in teams that include Principals (hosting and visiting), Curriculum Leaders, Teacher-Leaders (hosting and/or visiting) and District supervisory and/or support staff with visits to all classrooms.

Visit Protocol

Up-briefing with ALL participants (20 minutes)

- Host Principal and/or site Teacher-Leaders share highlights of the site professional development efforts from August to present.
- Host Principal shares either staff members' self-assessment of CCSS implementation strengths (e.g. "Making the Shift to Common Core - 2012/2013 School Implementation Rating") or their own assessment of the site's CCSS implementation strengths.

Classroom Visit Preparation with ALL participants (10 minutes)

- Host Principal shares the specific areas of focus for today's walk-through from the School Instructional Practice Implementation Tool in the areas of ELA, Math and/or Transitions in Pedagogy. The Host Principal will explain the specific expectations that have been communicated to staff in relation to the walk-through focus areas.
- The walk-through will include at least one Math focus area, one ELA focus area with optional consideration of one aspect of Transitions in Pedagogy among all of the classrooms that are visited.

Classroom Visits with ALL participants (up to 1 hour)

- Prior to entering classrooms, small walk-through groups will converse about what they expect to see and attempt to calibrate on the rating scale.
- Walk-through participants will visit all classrooms in small teams (2–4 participants per team) seeking positive examples of CCSS implementation efforts.
- Participants will collect data on the implementation data collection tool by plotting the degree of implementation observed on the continuum (e.g. one dot per classroom) and related evidence notes in the evidence column.

Group De-briefing and Summary Charting with ALL participants (up to 20 minutes)

- Upon return from classroom visits, participants will plot their visit data on a summary chart, creating a visual illustration.
- Small groups (ELA, Math and/or TiP) will share a summary of evidence collected and inferences generated to add to the summary chart.
- The participating group will have an opportunity to pose wonderings and/or open-ended questions to place on the summary chart and will conclude the whole-group portion of the visit by creating a celebratory visual representation that may be shared with staff.

Principal De-briefing with Host/Visiting Principals only

- As a walk-through team, Principals will complete the "next steps" column of the Summary Chart and discuss any collaborative efforts that might be supportive of the next steps.

Return Visit/Future Support

- Host Principal returns a copy or photo of the Summary Chart to his/her support provider.
- District supervisory staff may arrange to visit a staff meeting or write a statement of support that can be published to positively reinforce the school's efforts.

(Continued)

Figure 3.1 (Continued)

Supporting the Full Transition to Common Core State Standards Implementation Fall 2013		
Green Flags We'll know the CCSS for ELA/Literacy, Math and/or Transitions in Pedagogy are being implemented when...	Evidence observed or gathered 1= not observed at this time, 2 = little/no evidence at this time, 3 = some evidence at this time 4 = several examples of implementation observed 5 = multiple examples of implementation observed and this classroom practice is in place	
Area/s of Focus	**Findings**	**Evidence/Examples of Quality in Implementation**
K–2 ELA Today, students were engaged in systematic phonics instruction in a whole-group setting and then differentiated in small group instruction.	←→ 1 2 3 4 5	• Students were engaged in a whole-group lesson on the short /a/ sound. • In a small group, students were independently writing words with short /a/
3–8 ELA Today, students were asked to practice argumentative or informational/explanatory writing.	←→ 1 2 3 4 5	• Students were engaged in a discussion based upon the teacher's written model. In pairs, they discussed key aspects of the teacher's writing and how the written evidence related back to the text.

Supporting the Full Transition to Common Core State Standards Implementation Fall 2013		
Green Flags We'll know the CCSS for ELA/Literacy, Math and/or Transitions in Pedagogy are being implemented when...	Evidence observed or gathered 1= not observed at this time, 2 = little/no evidence at this time, 3 = some evidence at this time 4 = several examples of implementation observed 5 = multiple examples of implementation observed and this classroom practice is in place	
Area/s of Focus	**Findings**	**Evidence/Examples of Quality in Implementation**
K–8 Math Today, the teacher used Number Talks to help students gain computational fluency while thinking and talking like mathematicians and Talk Moves to encourage discussion and active listening.	← 1 2 3 4 5 →	• Students used Number Talks to demonstrate their "mental math" computation. Multiple students shared after wait time and then students used Talk Moves to further engage with the discussion. Four different Talk Moves were demonstrated across classrooms.
Transitions in Pedagogy – Optional Today, teachers experimented with having students state their learning targets at the onset of the ELA or Math lesson.	← 1 2 3 4 5 →	• All third grade students were practicing stating their learning targets during Math instruction.

Sample K–8 Focus Areas

(Continued)

Figure 3.1 (Continued)

Supporting the Full Transition to Common Core State Standards Implementation Fall 2013		
Green Flags We'll know the CCSS for ELA/Literacy, Math and/or Transitions in Pedagogy are being implemented when...	Evidence observed or gathered 1= not observed at this time, 2 = little/no evidence at this time, 3 = some evidence at this time 4 = several examples of implementation observed 5 = multiple examples of implementation observed and this classroom practice is in place	
Area/s of Focus	**Findings**	**Evidence/Examples of Quality in Implementation**
6–8 All subjects Today, in whole-group and small-group settings, students were listening, speaking and engaged in collaborative discussion to build on each other's observations or insights using evidence from the text and from using Thinking Maps. (WftBB = oral questions and open ended responses)	← → 1 2 3 4 5	• Students were observed collaboratively discussing evidence from the text. Each small group then organized its evidence onto a Thinking Map.
6–8 ELA Today, students were asked to practice argumentative or informational/explanatory writing.	← → 1 2 3 4 5	• Students were engaged in a discussion based upon the teacher's written model. In pairs, they discussed key aspects of the teacher's writing and how the written evidence related back to the text.

Supporting the Full Transition to Common Core State Standards Implementation
Fall 2013

Green Flags We'll know the CCSS for ELA/Literacy, Math and/or Transitions in Pedagogy are being implemented when...	Evidence observed or gathered 1= not observed at this time, 2 = little/no evidence at this time, 3 = some evidence at this time 4 = several examples of implementation observed 5 = multiple examples of implementation observed and this classroom practice is in place	
Area/s of Focus	**Findings**	**Evidence/Examples of Quality in Implementation**
6–8 Math Today, the teacher used Talk Moves to encourage discussion and active listening and to help students in thinking and talking like mathematicians.	←→ 1 2 3 4 5	• Students used Talk Moves to engage in student-to-student discussion, facilitated by the teacher. Four different Talk Moves were demonstrated across classrooms.
Transitions in Pedagogy Today, teachers experimented with having students state their learning targets at the onset of the ELA or Math lesson.	←→ 1 2 3 4 5	• All sixth grade students were practicing stating their learning targets during Math instruction.

Sample 6–8 Focus Areas

(Continued)

Figure 3.1 (Continued)

Supporting the Full Transition to Common Core State Standards Implementation Fall 2013		
Green Flags We'll know the CCSS for ELA/Literacy, Math and/or Transitions in Pedagogy are being implemented when...	Evidence observed or gathered 1= not observed at this time, 2 = little/no evidence at this time, 3 = some evidence at this time 4 = several examples of implementation observed 5 = multiple examples of implementation observed and this classroom practice is in place	
Area/s of Focus	**Findings**	**Evidence/Examples of Quality in Implementation**
ELA/Math/TIP	←→ 1 2 3 4 5	
ELA/Math/TIP	←→ 1 2 3 4 5	
ELA/Math/TIP	←→ 1 2 3 4 5	
ELA/Math/TIP	←→ 1 2 3 4 5	

Source: LBUSD. Used with permission.

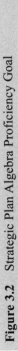

Figure 3.2 Strategic Plan Algebra Proficiency Goal

Long Beach Unified School District Strategic Plan, 2011–2016

Grade 8 Algebra Proficiency

Goal 1:

All students will attain proficiency in the core content areas.
Algebra Proficiency

Objective 1.3 & 1.4:

(1.3) To increase the percentage of 8th grade students enrolled in Algebra by 3% annually and (1.4) increase the percentage of 8th grade students who are proficient/advanced proficient by 1% and the percentage of 9th grade students who are proficient /advanced proficient by 2% annually.

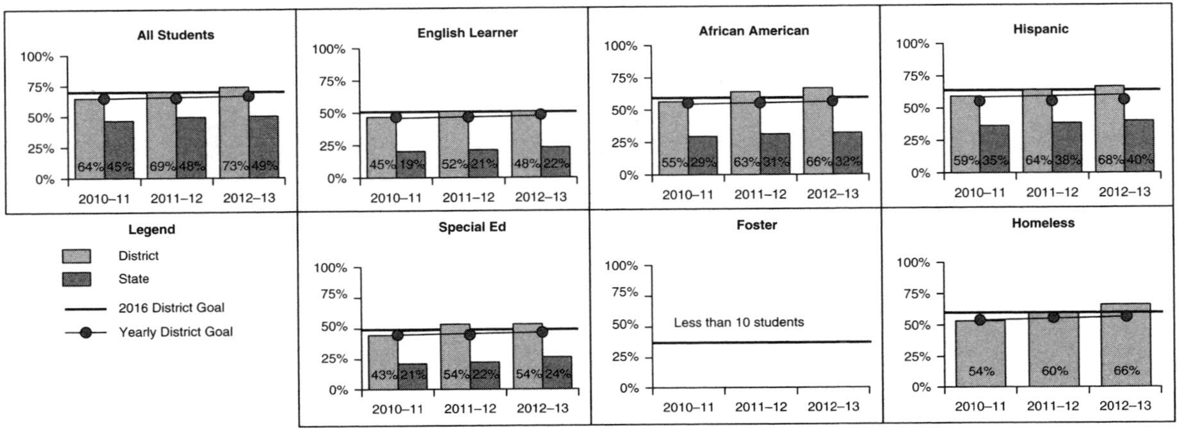

Source: LBUSD. Used with permission.

Index

CORWIN

A SAGE Company

The Corwin logo—a raven striding across an open book—represents the union of courage and learning. Corwin is committed to improving education for all learners by publishing books and other professional development resources for those serving the field of PreK–12 education. By providing practical, hands-on materials, Corwin continues to carry out the promise of its motto: **"Helping Educators Do Their Work Better."**

learningforward

Advancing professional learning for student success

Learning Forward (formerly National Staff Development Council) is an international association of learning educators committed to one purpose in K–12 education: Every educator engages in effective professional learning every day so every student achieves.